Y0-DNH-179

GOLD MIND

OPEN YOUR MIND;
CREATE YOUR WEALTH

GOLD MIND

OPEN YOUR MIND;
CREATE YOUR WEALTH

By kac young, DCH, RScM

Published by Marlene Morris Ministries, Inc.

Cover design: Marlene Morris
Back cover photo: Gloria Waco

ISBN 13: 978-0-9818368-1-2
ISBN 10: 0-9818368-1-x

First Printing June 2009

This book is lovingly dedicated
to my grandparents
Louis and Edith
and to my parents,
Vernon and Maureen,
for the invaluable information they shared with me.

Because of their examples I have been able to
create my own wealth
and sustain it.

For that, and so much more, I am deeply grateful.

The best thing we can do is
teach our children how to handle money

Benjamin Franklin

Acknowledgments

The author wishes to express her deepest gratitude to the following people who surely already know that they are shining jewels in the treasure chest of her life.

Marlene Morris, *Designer, Editor, Source of Inspiration, Advocate, Booster, Ally, Spiritual Philosopher, and Champion Extraordinaire.*

Terry Cole-Whittaker, *Gifted teacher and loving example of Spiritual Truth.*

Miss Jo Head, *Brilliant friend and Financial Warrior*

Peggy Jones, *the best friend anyone could ever have, a source of precious laughter, divine talent and uncanny support.*

Jerry Luedders, *Worker of Wonders and creator of Giant Leaps for those he touches.*

Jackie Zeman, *esteemed friend, colleague and shining example of human perfection.*

Ron Schultz, *known affectionately as Obi-Ron; a genuine social maverick*

Table of Contents

Forward

"The power of decision is your most valuable asset."

I have repeated these words to my daughters endlessly since the day they were born. Because I believe it's true. And because it took me a couple of decades of my life before I stumbled upon the realization of this truth.

Life is filled with limitless opportunities and possibilities. Yet the potential for change is a challenge which is easy to overlook.

Positive personal development can only happen when a person makes a conscious choice to change, to grow, to be different, and to become better than before. Self improvement requires commitment and a desire to let go of the old and make room for the new. Anyone can do it. All you need is a little unoccupied space and some directions.

This book is an easy to follow recipe which can and will change your way of thinking, doing and being. The results will change your life.

That's power.

I love this book. Enjoy!

Jacklyn Zeman

Jacklyn Zeman is one of the most recognized and well-liked actresses on television today. Well known to die-hard soap opera fans as nurse Bobbie Spencer, on ABC's daytime drama, General Hospital, Zeman is now in her 31st season, with more than 4,000 episodes to her credit. The recognition and accolades she has received for her philanthropic and humanitarian efforts are too numerous to list.

Author's Preface

As I write this book our country is experiencing a recession. Many have lost their homes, jobs, investments, plans and dreams for the future to a series of financial downturns and debacles that have left chasms where there were once hills of prosperity.

Daily we are challenged to remain strong and be creative in what appears to be a rampant reversal of fortune.

While the times may look and feel difficult, what we are actually experiencing is an adjustment in the balance of distribution. Many of us are being asked to reset the margins on our personal financial pages and to recreate the document of our wealth from scratch.

Gold Mind will show you exactly how to make that change in your life. Whether you are starting from scratch, recovering from portfolio losses, or are experiencing financial well-being, this book and the methods contained herein will help you to discover, maintain, and retain personal wealth.

You will learn how to mine the Gold Mind within and control the direction of your prosperity.

I didn't win the lottery, I didn't inherit my wealth, I lead an ordinary life, I had normal opportunities and I created a very comfortable pile of money and a great life-style by using The Money Model as my guide. Nothing fell from the sky, and no seven figure check ever arrived with a surprise knock at the door. Slow, steady, disciplined, and wise choices won this race - even in challenging financial times.

My purpose in writing this book is to pass along a body of information most of which I learned from others who were much wiser than I. They knew that the source of all wealth/ gold began in the mind. When applied, these lessons, principles and truths can turn your life into a profit center. They worked for me. All you really have to do is open up your own *Gold Mind.*

Gold Mind shows you how to prospect for your personal treasure. I enjoy a good life and I am both proud and thankful for what was taught to me. Now I pass what I learned along to you so you too may have a fruitful, abundant and secure life; and you can teach your children the same lessons.

No one should have to live with the stress of financial lack. We can all be abundant - no matter who we are, or what is going on; in spite of what may appear to be beyond our immediate control.

The Greatest good you can do for another is not just
to share your riches, but to reveal to him his own.
Benjamin Disraeli

Introduction
(Do not skip over this!)

There have always been those who stayed awake at night worrying about how they were going to pay the mortgage.

Today, the financial situation we call a recession, has raised the world-wide insomnia level to pandemic proportions.

It's not that I never lose sleep over money matters, even with all my understanding, I can still be surprised by the whims of a manic market or a notice from the Internal Revenue Service. But, if I am laying awake in the middle of the night I'm not counting sheep, or tossing and turning; I'm being productive - I'm mining for gold.

In times when finances are in flux and many people are feeling the effects of the adjustment, we have to readjust our thinking and our patterns and establish, or reestablish, a firm foundation for the future. Especially in times of change, it is important to look deeply into all that we hold dear and commit to a fresh start. No matter what your financial situation, the lessons in this book will change your life if you are willing to put in some effort.

Mining can be a messy business at first, but in the end you will have your own stash of gold to enjoy.

Currently our educational systems don't teach us what we *really* need to know about money. They teach us a great deal about how to add numbers and move decimal points, but they don't teach us one single syllable about cash-flow and smart money management. Unless you went to business school, or unless you had parents who taught you about the value of money, and the art of wisely managing your resources (and most of them probably didn't because they didn't really understand it fully themselves), then you haven't been taught what you absolutely need to know.

I have spent decades watching people waste their money because they didn't know what to do with it or how to manage their finances. For a lot of them money was just "there" or

1

"not there" as the case might be. A dear friend once actually said, "As long as I still have checks in my wallet, I'll keep writing them."

As amusing as that phrase may be, it is also the core reason for much unhappiness and many foreclosures. We make money, but we don't fully understand the nature of it, and we don't manage it; not because there is something intrinsically wrong with us, but because we don't know how to. And, we don't know, or we've forgotten, that our minds are a natural source of riches. Our gold lies within us.

I am no different than anyone else in most of the important ways, or in terms of special opportunities. However I am different than most of my contemporaries in one very important way: as a child my father taught me about the nature and value of money; how to acquire it, what to do with it, what to think about it, how to respect it (and what it could do to enhance my life), how to manage it wisely, and how to cherish it.

It's never too late! I want you to learn the rules I learned, and I want you to *teach them to your children* so that they may have the financial platform to support their lives, families and greatest desires. I want everyone I know and love to live on a solid financial foundation and to really understand how money works at the core of his or her being. I want *everyone* to know these truths, secrets, principles and practices so we can all have what we need to live our precious lives to the fullest and not worry about it.

I know my financial well-being (my Gold) depends on my mental outlook (my Mind). If I think on the right things, I will be led to the right actions; action which will create, maintain and retain my wealth.

Regardless of your past understanding, or misunderstanding, and experience, what I absolutely know is that there is a *financial genius* within you – waiting to step up and take charge of your life and treasure. There is no magic pill, there is no fairy wand, there is no spell, (although I believe you can purchase one on the Internet for $99.00), but there *are* Principles, spiritual laws, guidelines, and patterns you can come to understand and establish that will attract the financial security you want for your future. Practice these and you'll have peace of mind and you'll have dreams that actually do come true.

There is a gold mine of plenty waiting for you to claim it - in spite of what the media says. You can have and sustain wealth. That's why I've written this book.

Put on your imaginary miner's cap; we're going in!

My aim is not to teach the method that everyone ought to follow to conduct his reason well, but solely to reveal how I have tried to conduct my own.
-Rene Descartes.

Chapter One
Back to (Home) School

The memory of childhood is so rich
it takes a lifetime to unpack.
– John O'Donohue

It all begins at home. Your young (potentially gold) mind was the unconscious slate onto which your role models (usually your parents) wrote your first concepts about money. The patterns they played out deeply engraved your personal thoughts about money. And, what you think about money leads to your feelings about it.

Accompanying each of your thoughts are feelings. Your feelings demonstrate the beliefs you hold about money today. Those feelings, primarily at the unconscious level, control how you acquire your money and what you do with the money you receive. If you're given a dollar, your subconscious feeling patterns will tell you what to do with that dollar. Until you take control of your feelings, you'll never be in control of your money. *Never.*

Reread that paragraph. Your key to success lies in your understanding of those 5 sentences.

You're probably familiar with the television commercial that asks, "What's in your wallet?" The real question to ask is: "What's in your *mind* about what's in your wallet?" When you seriously ask yourself that question you unearth the true roots of what you believe about money. As you come to know your deep-seated thoughts about money you can begin to shift the reality of how it behaves in your life. You will not be able to change your relationship with money until you know what you *think, feel* and *believe* about it under the surface. You can't make a change until you have gathered all of the evidence and examined it thoroughly. You have to be a bit of a detective to maneuver around the obvious and delve into the nebulous and often thorny territory of your hidden beliefs. But this is where the Gold is hidden - in your beliefs. The first step in mining is assessing what you have to work with before you start digging in.

You can't be blamed for what you currently think and feel about money. If this is the first time you've questioned your beliefs, remember, you didn't create those first impressions alone; you had a lot of help. You began your journey from the central heartbeat of your family unit. For better or worse, your relationship with money is the result of what those first impressions were. In order to change those impressions you will need to take a few moments and make a short journey back to your early years to view the patterns that shaped your beliefs. Together, let's discover what we have to work with.

The goal of this exercise is to locate the origins of your thoughts about money by looking into your early family trends; it is not to place blame or find fault with anyone. This exercise is about fact finding, not fault finding. Later on we will mine the gold we find in this exercise. Please answer the following questions either in your mind, or on paper if you choose.

As A Child:

Who was the primary income earner in your family?
Did both parents contribute to family finances?
Was there one parent who dispersed the income?
In your family was there a system of balancing income with outflow?
Did your parental model use any system for budgeting?
Were you aware of where the money for your family came from?
Was money management an organized effort, or was it more of a random event?
(In other words was there a specific time for paying bills, were they paid as they came in, or were bills stuffed into a drawer and dealt with as money showed up?)
Were the children made aware of family finances or did the adults handle everything quietly?
Were money and finances discussed openly?
Did you have an allowance growing up?
Were any chores required of you in exchange for money?
Who kept the house clean?
Who did the grocery shopping?

Did the children share in the home care and maintenance?

Was there a joint account for managing family expenses?

Did you know what utilities were and how much they cost?

How were gifts handled in your home? (Did you get everything you wanted for holidays and birthdays or did you have to wait?)

Did you have health coverage growing up?

Did you attend private or public school?

How did your family handle financial emergencies?

Was there a safety net or a savings account for unplanned expenditures?

Did your family take regular vacations?

Did you know vacations were planned and paid for?

Did your parents use credit cards? If so, were you aware of the amount of debt they carried?

Did you know how much your house cost? Or, what the monthly rent was?

Was there ever bickering about money in your household?

Can you recall a positive memory about money from your childhood?

Do you have a negative memory about money from your childhood?

As A Teenager:

How did you receive your spending money?

Were you encouraged to earn your own spending money?

Did you have a job?

Did your siblings have jobs?

How did you handle your own money?

Did your parents pay for every event you wanted to attend?

Did you have a specific amount of money that you were asked to manage?

Did you have a savings account?

What was the first account you ever opened in your own name? How old were you?

How did your best friend(s) handle money?

Were there things you couldn't do, events you couldn't attend, or desires you couldn't support due to lack of money?

Were you ever embarrassed about money issues?

Was your embarrassment primarily due to your parent's money situation or your own?

Is there a memory about money that really stands out in your mind from your teenage years?

Today:

Are you comfortable or uncomfortable with the subject of money?

Do you always have enough money to cover your expenses?

Do you ever have enough?

Do you live on credit cards?

Do you plan ahead for birthday and holiday gifts, or do you buy at the last moment?

Do you have a working budget for your income?

Do you know how to allocate your monthly expenses?

How do you handle the utility bills as they rise and fall seasonally?

Do you purchase items for yourself with a plan in mind, or do you impulse buy?

Do you purchase groceries based on a predetermined menu plan? Or, do you just buy what you feel like buying when you're in the store?

What is the most imprudent thing you've ever done with money?

What is the smartest thing you've ever done with money?

Do you trust yourself to manage money?

Are you afraid of money?

Are you afraid of the lack of money?

Do you have an emergency account in case you need cash immediately?

Do you have a retirement account?

Is that account from your employer, or do you have an independent account into which you contribute annually?

Do you have a will or a living trust?

Do you have life insurance?
Do you have health insurance?
What is the first thing you would do if someone handed you one million dollars?
If there was one thing you could change in your financial life, what would it be?
What is the second thing you would change?

Answering these questions will help you to access your subconscious mind and shake loose some of those ingrained attitudes about money that you may not be aware even exist. It is imperative that you identify both the positive thoughts as well as the negative. Positive thoughts assist you in your financial life; negative ones are the invisible bands which hold you back from an affirming and healthy relationship with money. The gold will surface when we clear away the rocks that block our access.

Did anything surprise you? What did you learn about yourself?

You came into the world as a clean slate, impressionable and unwritten. Beliefs and attitudes were passed down to you from your parents and elders. Unless you have previously reviewed and dissected your relationship with money, you are probably operating from conditioning, not conscious creation. Becoming aware of your pre-conditioned thinking sets the stage for you to create your own beliefs according to what you want to be and have.

If you skipped the exercise in this chapter, go back and do it now. You must understand what you're working with, before you can begin to change it. If you want to achieve wealth, do the work; otherwise this book will be pleasant entertainment but not a tool for permanent change.

All glory comes from daring to begin.
– Anonymous

Chapter Two
Lesson 1:
44 Acres of Gold

> *Look deep into Nature and then*
> *you will understand everything better.*
> –Albert Einstein

I was one of the lucky ones. I had a great money model to follow. My father taught me the value of money early on. I grew up observing how the family money was managed, how it was treated with great respect and how it was absolutely never taken for granted.

It began when my American grandparents, Louis and Edith, ran away from home at the age of nineteen to get married. They had no financial reserves behind them, but they wanted to be together so they eloped; much against the wishes of my grandmother's stern Nordic mother. As newlyweds they built their own log cabin. My grandfather had quit school at the age of 14 out of necessity, to support his mother and siblings. His dad, a jeweler from Boston, left the family abruptly and, being the oldest son, young Louis became the sole support of his abandoned family by default. He learned building trades at the hands of local craftsmen and, by the time he met and married my grandmother, he was proficient enough to build their first home out of freshly milled logs - with her indefatigable help. She was all of 5 feet tall and weighed about 100 pounds, but together they built their home from the foundation up; and were proud and content living in Elk River, Idaho.

As they prospered they moved to Potlach, Idaho where they purchased land and built a modest farmhouse. My father grew up farming that land with my grandfather. Grandad held down a full time job as head electrician for the Potlach Forest Mills, but after work and on weekends he planted, tended, and harvested his 44 acres of wheat. Grandmother cooked, baked, sewed, canned the fruits and vegetables she grew on the land, kept the house immaculate, and tended the animals they raised. Each year my father and grandfather harvested those precious 44 acres of golden wheat and trucked them into town for sale. They both understood that by working two jobs and having two streams of income, they would climb higher on the ladder of financial success. If the crops were lean one year, the second job saw them through. If there was a bumper crop another year, the proceeds went into a fund to balance out the inevitable lean times. It was a financial rhythm as dependable and reliable as the ebb and flow of the sea.

My father had a wonderful model to follow. He learned from *his* father how to balance the lean years with the plenty. He also learned it from the land. One year the land might give forth a bounteous crop; the next year might be far more frugal due to pests, weather or fire. The family had to work with reserves in order to withstand what nature might hand them. They kept a back-up supply of money, a supply of seed and a big tank of water to bridge the gaps. Grandad had no model to follow. He had to learn from any source willing to teach. His greatest teacher was Nature herself.

Nature is a brilliant master teacher. Contained within her periodic cycles is everything that we need to learn about survival and thriving. Some years she extends plenty of everything; plenty of water, an abundance of sunlight, ample rain, generous weather and favorable seasons. Some years she brings the opposite: fires that destroy, floods that drown, pestilence that devours, winds that uproot, toxins that kill, and climatic conditions that annihilate even the hardiest of plantings. No being can stand against the forces of Nature when she performs. The only chance for success one has in the face of these dynamic variances is the art and science of *resource management*.

My grandfather and my father were excellent managers of their assets. They were dedicated and humble students of capricious Creation and they passed along some of those practices to me. I didn't have to build my own log cabin, but I did practice what they taught me, and because of that I am able to weather the financial storms of my life, as well as harvesting the bounty in the bumper years. I am deeply grateful for their legacy. From their example, I learned how to mine for gold and how to store it, should there come a day when the mine gave out.

The first thing you have to learn about money is that it is a medium of trade, *and* it is something more. Our exploration into the true nature of money begins with a short history lesson.

Dutch Colonial Director General, Peter Minuit purchased the island of Manhattan from the Lenape Native Americans in 1626 for $24 worth of glass beads. On the surface that wasn't such a great deal, at least not for the Native Americans. Prior to trading with the Dutch, the only Lenape trading experience was with other Native American and Native Canadian tribes. Their method of exchange was wampum. Wampum were hand made ornamental belts featuring purple and white mollusk shells.

The Lenape had no metal tools, they harvested the mollusks by hand and by diving - without the aid of scuba gear. These hand crafted belts were treasured by other tribes, like gold would be to us. In that culture the wampum held great value. When the Dutch traded European-made metal tools to them the Lenape thought they'd made it big. Suddenly the harvest was much easier and they were able to haul in a ton of mollusks, but when the mollusks became easy to obtain and so plentiful, their value declined. The greater the supply, the less the demand. The Lenape were caught off-guard about the deflated value of the shells, so to compensate for the loss in income they went into beaver trapping and pelt-pushing. Within two years the beaver population was reduced to a dismal few and the Lenape were once again at the mercy of the buyers. They couldn't meet the demand for their product because the supply had dwindled, so those who survived moved west. The Lenape went from 15,000 to 200 over the next decade.

You are probably wondering why you are reading about the Lenape Clan when what you really want to learn is how to handle your own finances. This is your first lesson. The moral of this story is: Not planning ahead and not understanding how *value* works can make anybody's wampum worthless overnight. Unlike my grandfather who knew to store up his earnings or his crops for the lean years, the Lenape didn't *and* they perished because of it.

So, what about you? What is your wampum? What are you trading in exchange for what you need? What value do you place on your wampum? Is your wampum something you take for granted, or do you treat it like a natural resource and practice wise conservation?

Wampum, or its equivalent, was invented by our ancestors because they needed to have some kind of way to get or trade something that they wanted from someone else who had it. Remember you came into this world wampum-free, without one unit of exchange, and then what happened? Do you recall the first time you held money in your hand? Let's do this little exercise on our search for the treasure we can mine later on.

Exercise # 1

> Take a moment, close your eyes, and think back to your earliest memory about money. Just relax. The memory will come. Was the money a gift? Did you earn it? Was it an allowance? Did you find it on the street? Recall your first emotion about having money in your possession. How did you feel about it? Describe your feelings to yourself, or write them down if you wish.

When I was a young whippersnapper[1] my Grandad used to give me quarters and packages of M&M's. My first association with money was a sweet one!

Your first memory of money is embedded within you and affects you to this day. Your recollection can give you even more insight.

Exercise #2

> Close your eyes again and bring back your first memory of money. Allow the past to enlighten you. What happened next? Recall what you did with that money. Do not make a value judgment about the action, simply remember what it was and what you did with it.

---

[1] *Old-fashioned term meaning* a young impertinent overconfident person. C'est moi!

When we receive money we have ultimate and total choice over our actions with it. If you are thinking, "No I don't have a choice, I *have* to pay my rent, I have a car payment, I have groceries to buy," erase that thought from your mind. You *do* have a choice. That's the point of the 2nd exercise. You have choice. Choice is the key to having your money propel you or to you being the one in charge.

> *Do you live paycheck to paycheck?*
> *Do you have a savings account or a piggy bank that grows and that you don't raid at least once a year?*
> *Are you willing to be thrilled at the sight of interest gained as opposed to finance charges?*
> *Are you prepared for the lean years, or are you living like the good years will never end?*

I am not suggesting that you live life in fear of "rainy days" but I am encouraging you to live in accordance with natural cycles that bring both *rain and drought*. You can count on Nature to be unpredictable, therefore you must carefully plan ahead in order to withstand the natural forces of supply and shortfall. The idea is to move in congruence with the forces as they change from one year to the next; not contest them, rail against them, or be crushed and ruined by them. Instead, acknowledge them, and work with them. *"How do we do that?"* The answers await you in the following chapters. You'll have a Money Model to follow and there is a natural progression that will serve you well.

Anticipate the difficult by managing the easy.
–Lao Tzu

Chapter Three
Lesson 2:
The Roaring Twenties

People, even more than things, have to be restored,
renewed, revived, reclaimed, and redeemed;
never throw out anyone. [1]
– Audrey Hepburn

It was the second half of the twentieth century. Four young women in their twenties were just starting out in their careers. Their education and intelligence put the friends on equal footing as they entered the job market. All four of them landed good jobs and were making roughly the same income. Yet, today only two of them are financially stable and secure. They all had to weather strong markets and weak markets. They all had equal opportunities and very similar incomes. What happened? Why did two end up well-off and the other two not? The answer lies in the choices they made about what they did with their money when they got it. Perhaps through their stories we can figure out what didn't work well for two of them.

Let's call the friends Sarah, Marie, Angela and Zelda. Sarah and Marie had luxurious, sunny apartments downtown in the city. Angela shared an apartment with a roommate who paid half the rent. Zelda lived alone in a nice, safe, but older neighborhood, in the suburbs, and paid one-third the rent that Sarah and Marie paid. Sarah and Marie usually attended movies on the weekends, went out to dinner several nights a week, and had payments for snazzy cars they thought made them look sleek and sexy. They frequently shopped at the mall and always looked chic - with only an occasional splurge at Saks Fifth Avenue. Their handbags matched their shoes and they wore the most up–to-date costume jewelry. They subscribed to the latest and greatest magazines and got regular manicures. Oh and, they *loved* to valet park; it was the ultimate symbol of luxury for them.

Angela worked as an aerobics instructor and a personal trainer during the day and took free-lance bookkeeping jobs at night and on weekends. She joined Sarah and Marie for movies and

[1] This means you, too!

parties when she chose to, but she also put much of her cash aside. Zelda did not join her friends very often. She didn't choose to splurge on pricey restaurants, and she preferred having her biggest meal at lunch, when the prices were lower. She also had a preference for eating lighter at night and she liked her evenings at home.

Sarah and Marie loved being able to say they had eaten at "this or that" restaurant in trendy places where they could be "seen." They had lots of fun, paid lots of valets lots of money, and could always tell their friends about the hottest and hippest five-star restaurants they had been to. Meanwhile, Zelda joined them occasionally, but usually not at the more expensive places. Often she choose to meet up with them for a movie *after* the meal and she always parked her own car and walked a distance to the event - avoiding the valet parking charges. Oh, make no mistake, Zelda had plenty of fun; she just didn't spend as much.

Zelda didn't suffer for lack of a social life. Her life was full, busy and productive. She invited friends to her apartment for dinner, frequented art fairs, took day-trips to the woods but also she spent a lot of time adding to the knowledge-base of her job, observing those more skilled, and in general developing herself professionally by studying evenings and weekends on her own time.

Sarah and Marie spent a lot of time at the mall. Sarah loved blazers and jackets and acquired them as one would buy chicken eggs - by the dozen. She enjoyed wearing the trendy jewelry shown in her magazines. Marie was much the same, although she did like to take advantage of the prices at wholesale and discount stores. Angela loved the upscale re-sale boutiques and spent a few of her days-off on the wealthy side of town looking for top quality clothing at bargain prices. Zelda only bought genuine jewelry, on sale. She may not have had the "latest fashion look" but her accessories were top quality and would stand the test of time. When her friends were throwing out their out-of-style baubles, Zelda continued to wear the Real McCoy.

Angela bought a condo with the money she saved from her odd jobs and tips. Having a roommate and sharing the cost of rent and utilities reduced her overhead. When she scoured the neighborhood and found an apartment complex "going condo" she tallied up her assets and decided to take the plunge. She also invited her roommate along. Not only was she able to afford the payments, but she had someone to share the burden and the utilities as well. Angela was smart. She rightly figured that the roommate's share of the rent would cover the mortgage payment and part of the condo fees. Angela was responsible for the property taxes and maintenance repairs. She took her original rent money and placed it in a special savings account "as if" she were paying rent. Any extra cash she got, she put into this account. She continued to work as a fitness trainer and also to save up for her greatest love: travel.

While her friends paid larger rents, by the time she was thirty, Zelda had saved enough money to put a down payment on a substantial house. Her mortgage payment equaled her friends' rent, but the tax benefits of home ownership far outweighed those of renting. Sarah and Marie were flabbergasted. "How can she afford a house like that?" they whispered to each other. Zelda knew they could have the same situation if only they were willing to make some trade-offs. It never crossed their minds. They loved their lives and they weren't going to stop living them the way they wanted to. They just didn't understand why they couldn't have it all!

Sarah was successful in her work. She made a very decent living as a photographer, worked for some of the best companies and, like Angela, also loved to travel. Sarah seemed to be on a plane to New York, London, Las Vegas or Italy every other month. She took several cruises and even managed to make a few voyages complimentary by enlisting other passengers for cruise lines. Sometimes she took pictures or taught photography classes in exchange for passage.

Midway through her career Sarah also purchased a condo. She paid more for it (due to inflation) than Angela and Zelda had paid for their respective real estate because she got in the game later than they did. Nonetheless, she did convert her rent money into mortgage payments thus protecting her assets over time.

Marie, who worked in marketing and public relations, never chose to do that. She always rented. She rented bigger and better apartments, then bigger and better houses. She became a perennial renter.

What do you think happened to our friends when they got into their fifties? I'll tell you: Two are still working and living paycheck to paycheck; taking jobs they may not necessarily want to take in order to pay bills. Angela is doing what she loves to do, travel. She does not travel first class by any means, but she has seen the world six times over and has had more experience in one lifetime than most of us would have in twenty. In order to finance her dreams she has learned to be thrifty, cautious and clever with her money. The condo she purchased in her thirties sold for a nice 300% profit and the proceeds allow her to live frugally and travel constantly without needing to earn a weekly paycheck.

Zelda paid $250,000 for a home that she is on the market 25 years later at a profit of 500%. It was her plan all along not to have a mortgage. She paid-down the principle over the course of ten years by adding more and more money to the monthly payment as her income level rose. By the time she was ready to sell her home, no bank held a mortgage and the entire proceeds from the sale could go into her portfolio. She'll live quite comfortably on the proceeds from the sale of the house and the interest on the savings she was able to store away throughout the years. She can easily afford five-star restaurants, but still chooses to do so only on special occasions. What was the magic formula? Did Angela and Zelda just *get lucky* or was there a plan, a program, and a process that led them into financial comfort?

At this point it probably won't surprise you to learn that I am "Zelda". And I want to communicate the thinking, the beliefs, and the actions that led me into financial security. I have a quality of life today that allows me to be the driver and not the driven. If you were not taught the basics, and if you are living like Sarah and Marie and always scrambling for the next rent check, then please allow me to teach you what I was taught so you can apply the same formula to your life and end up able to afford your dreams and enjoy financial peace of mind in your later years.

The point of this story was to illustrate the choices we make while having similar opportunities. Some make choices in the moment for the future; others make choices for the moment. The results speak for themselves. What results do you want to have? What depths are you willing to probe? What choices are you willing to make to have prosperity?

Let's make sure you have some strong concepts in your Gold Mind before we do anything else.

It's not our mistakes that define us;
it's what we do afterwards.
Numbers (Television Production)

Chapter Four
Lesson 3:
The Money Model

Cherish your visions and your dreams
as they are the children of your soul,
the blueprints of your ultimate achievement.
– Napoleon Hill

Many people throw the word "prosperity" around without having one clue as to what it really means. For some "experts" it means nothing more than a way to get inside *your* wallet. They are making money because they have coaxed you into believing they have something to share. At the risk of offending those of you who have already bought into their hype: Most of them do not.

In the last chapter you met Sarah, Marie, Angela and me, "Zelda." (I like the name so I'm keeping it for now.) You also learned a good deal about what each of them really *valued* and how that shaped their financial future. Value is just one of the key factors in creating financial happiness; there are several other areas as well.

In spite of what many money gurus may claim, there is no magic or secret formula for attaining financial freedom and stability. There is however, a model to follow if you want to insure your future financial success. There are nine qualities, nine areas of consideration, that make up The Money Model.

Understanding
Value
Principles
Acquisition
Discipline
Exchange
Management
Contribution
Balance

For the sake of illustration, I'll use examples from our four friends in the last chapter to clarify some of these areas.

Understanding is the very personal combination of your past beliefs (B) and your current actions (A) which equals your financial status. Or, to put it mathematically, $A+B=\$\$\$$. (Sarah believed that you could spend everything you made. Marie believed you could spend as long as you still had checks in your checkbook. Angela believed that you should spend far less than you made and save for what you really want, and Zelda believed that you follow a percentage program for spending and curtail frivolous expenses for the first few decades of your life.) Understanding, then, is a combination of what you think about money, what you think money *is*, where it comes *from*, and what you believe you ought to be able to *do* with it. What is in your mind about money? How does it come to you and what do you do with it when you have it?

Value is what society at large considers the rate of exchange to be and, more importantly, what *you* believe to be worthy of spending your time and money on. (Sarah believed being in the vicinity of the rich and famous was of great value; Marie believed that tomorrow would be another day - and she might just win the lotto anyway, so why not purchase those designer shoes now; Angela believed she could get a better deal, negotiate a lower price, or find an outlet supply for what she wanted and needed. Zelda considered freedom and financial security the biggest assets and valued money for the amount of personal freedom they could supply.)

Principles are non-discriminatory invisible laws that always remain the same. Principles are eternal and neutral. They have worked the same way for as long as the Universe has been in existence, and they will continue to operate powerfully, uniformly and invisibly for the rest of time. They can neither be created nor destroyed, like gravity, they just are. (Sarah thinks principles are boring; Marie believes her pastor should abide by them. Angela doesn't think much about them but uses them anyway; Zelda is always looking for new ways to practice the principles, especially the money principles, she understands.) You can understand and use them too.

Acquisition is defined as the action of money coming into your life and the means by which you attain that inflow. (Sarah thinks this applies to her next paycheck; Marie believes you go where you can make the best and quickest buck; Angela works hard and is careful to notice how much interest her savings make; and Zelda closely observes both what her income and what her acquisitions are earning.)

Discipline refers to the intentions we have, and the actions we are willing to take, in order to preserve what we acquire. Discipline is the method by which we bring order into our personal world and the systems we set in motion to govern our financial behavior. Discipline doesn't have to be ugly, hard or scary. It doesn't even have to be difficult, it just has to be followed. (Sarah believes that discipline means not eating bread with your meal; Marie thinks it means limiting her purchases to four pair of shoes at the two-for-one special; Angela is just as happy buying knock-offs instead of the real thing; and Zelda pays cash for everything and settles up every bill at the end of each month.)

Exchange shows how we give and take from the Universal pool of money and abundance. It is both a verb and a noun, so it refers to the exchange of one thing for another *and* it refers to the physical coin of the realm. (Sarah thinks exchange is something you do with a foreign currency at an airport; Marie believes in taking back unwanted Christmas or birthday presents and getting cash; Angela barters and is generous with her time in exchange for clothes and vacations; Zelda places value on everything she gives, receives, does and accepts.)

Management is the system we use to apportion our money and the thinking behind it. This is a set of pre-established standards combined with a designed methodology for spending. (Sarah believes management is an unnecessary infringement on her self-expression; Marie believes it's the landlord; Angela is too busy doing it naturally to think much about it; and Zelda operates instinctively in an auto-pilot management formula that she learned as a wee tot.)

Contribution is what we bring to the world in the form of our gifts and talents. It also defines the essential giving-back, and activity of charity, which we all must do in order to foster global prosperity and maintain our integrity as participants in the spectrum of life. (Sarah mostly contributes to herself and her needs; Marie usually doesn't have any spare change around, but will gladly help you out if you need anything; Angela gives more of her time than cash; and Zelda believes in giving 10% of her time and 10% of her earnings to the sources of her spiritual inspiration and to those who contribute to her soul's expansion; even when times are tough.)

Balance means how we keep our money, our health, our loves, our work, our desires, our dreams and our entire life not only in perspective but also in harmony. (Sarah thinks balance is a gymnastic sport at the Olympics, or something a seal does with a ball on it's nose; Marie is afraid of the word because she thinks it might have something to do with her checking account; Angela eats when she's hungry and sleeps when she's tried and can't wait for her next trip overseas; Zelda skillfully walks a balance beam when times are lean, and swings in the hammock when there is plenty.) It is an ongoing challenge to have and to maintain this mercurial quality when the world is changing faster than one can keep pace. However this skill is essential for those who wish to succeed.

The Money Model[1] on the following page is a tool for organizing all of these elements in your thinking and a beginning place from which you will create financial balance and prosperity in your mind.

In the next chapters we'll explore the nine areas of the Money Model. Our goal is to get all of the areas into practice and balance. When all nine are working together and nourishing each other there is prosperity in your life and sound sleep in your nights. Let me show you each of these works individually and then collectively, as a unit.

---

[1] See Appendix A for a detailed history of the Money Model.

The Money Model

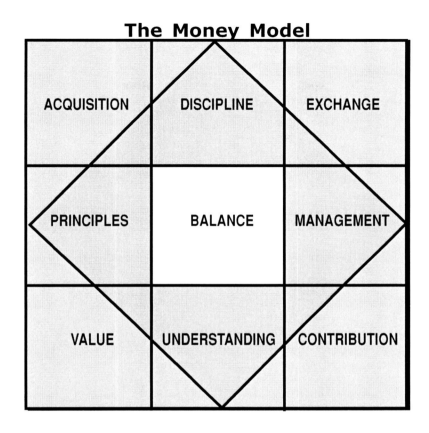

ACQUISITION	DISCIPLINE	EXCHANGE
PRINCIPLES	BALANCE	MANAGEMENT
VALUE	UNDERSTANDING	CONTRIBUTION

There are a total of nine squares in The Money Model. Consider them as you would a board game. You begin with the square of *Understanding* and progress clockwise around the path just as you do in your life; one step at a time. *Understanding* is the first form of knowledge. Once you understand something you consciously, or unconsciously, place *Value* on it. Based on how you value something, it becomes important to you, or it does not.

From *Value* you move onto *Principles*, where you learn to play according to the rules: yours and the Universe's. You continually absorb life-lessons as you progress around the square. *Principles* shape your journey; the more you know about them, and the more you practice living and working with them, the more you will achieve and gain. There's much more ahead about *Principles*.

27

Move up one step and *Principles* leads you directly to *Acquisition*. Through your conscious or unconscious use of principles, you acquire life experiences, skills and possessions. The degree of conscious use determines the quantity and quality of your acquisitions. In the next square, *Discipline*, you begin to categorize and prioritize what you acquire. *Discipline* is a practice as well as an action. In and through *Discipline* you begin to grow and design your prosperity.

Are you starting to see to see the relationship each square has to another?

Moving into *Exchange* you learn how to parlay your acquisitions and trade with others. You also learn, via *Discipline*, what to exchange and what to retain for your life. Moving on from *Exchange*, you step into the *Management* of the acquisitions that you have attained. This square provides you the techniques and methods by which you will increase or decrease, and distribute your holdings. *Contribution* is next and completes your journey around the perimeter of the square. Giving back generously and sustaining your source of supply is the key to having more. At the center of the Money Model, touching all the other squares is *Balance*. This square provides stability for the entire model and holds the clear purpose and intention of your life and its abundance. Again, our goal is to organize all of the facets of your life so they can work together, support and influence each other. When we achieve *Balance* in all nine areas we have successfully mined our Gold.

In the next chapter we will examine all nine squares in depth investigating the importance and vitality of each one. The squares of The Money Model are your stepping stones to wealth. Contained within each of them are secrets that will change your life.

If one advances confidently in the direction of his dreams,
and endeavors to live the life which he has imagined
he will meet with success.
– Henry David Thoreau

Chapter Five
Lesson 4:
The Money Model Square by Square

The noblest pleasure is the joy of understanding.
– Leonardo da Vinci

In the previous chapter you were introduced to the power in the nine squares of The Money Model. These are areas for mastering what you think about money now. In this chapter we enter into the nitty-gritty business of becoming rich. Though it might look like one of them, this isn't a board game; it's the blueprint to creating your financial future in a very new and solid way. Take notes and allow this information to replace any old beliefs you have about money. These concepts will transform your future.

Let's start with **Understanding:** Your past beliefs (B) combined with your current actions (A) equals your financial status. Or, to put it mathematically: A+B=$$$.

There is a great difference between knowing and understanding: you can know a lot about something and not really understand it.
– Charles F. Kettering

We may think we know a lot about money: The nightly news reports the box office totals of the weekend movie releases; we learn the annual salary of American Idol's Simon Cowell from host Ryan Seacrest[1]; we follow Martha Stewart's saga when she does time in prison because of a money related insider's deal; and we believe that we'd be much happier if we suddenly won the lotto and had a windfall of it. But the real question is, *Would we really be happier?* We *might* be, if we had an understanding of what money truly is and how it works. But most of us do not; we just *think* we do. There are two sides of money. It is a viable medium of trade, *and* there is something more to it!

The first thing we have to do is to define what we mean by "money". Remember the Lenape Clan from Chapter Two? The moral of their story was that not planning ahead and not

---

[1] American Idol, Season 7, 2008

understanding how money and value work together can make anybody's wampum worthless overnight. The Lenape clearly didn't understand. Their story could have had a different ending altogether if they'd known and understood more about their relationship to their wampum and the value they attached to it; or what they "thought" the value was. Ignorance and greed eventually got the best of them.

Generally, we understand that money is a thing and that we can do something with it once we get it. It is a means to an end and, between here and there, we have choices to make. What are we going to do with it once we have it and how will we choose to use it? Dollars, whether they are windfalls or exchanged for our labors, are our wampum.

But there is a depth to understanding money that reaches far beyond the physical. It has to do with the spiritual significance of money. We mustn't just settle for what we can see and touch; we must explore the deeper, more archetypal and invisible layers of understanding if we are to make lasting changes.

We live in a physical world, yet we *operate* on an invisible one. The key is to include each of these in our understanding and awareness.

In his masterpiece of sound spiritual and financial advice, Spiritual Economics, Eric Butterworth writes:

> *The word affluence is an overworked word in our time, usually implying cars and houses and baubles of all kinds. Its literal meaning is "an abundant flow" and not things at all. When we are consciously centered in the universal flow, we experience inner direction and the unfoldment of creative activity. Things come too, but prosperity is not just having things. It is the consciousness that attracts things.*

Consciousness. Money is consciousness in action. If you think about it, money was *invented* as a means of convenient exchange. It *first began* as an idea and then *became* a thing. Early humans needed to solve a problem: *How do I get some of what you have?* The answer came in the form of a thought,

What if I traded you something I have for what you have? And then early beings acted upon that thought and began trading one thing for another. Soon the need for order and organization arose, so that a form of currency was agreed upon as the medium of exchange. It was easier to exchange clam shells, which fit in your pocket, than to carry around a cash cow, which didn't. Next, banks were invented. After all now that there was a convenient medium of exchange, where were you to keep it? The cow went back into the barn and the money went into the bank, of course. Clam shells and cows were the original "gold".

> *The imagination is literally the workshop wherein are fashioned all plans created by man.*
> – Napoleon Hill

Underlying all sense of trade is the concept of flow. Something flows out and something else flows in. I learned from the great spiritual teacher Terry Cole-Whittaker that our abundance is similar to a water pipe that is continually full of water. It's always there. It's always ready to give us what we need. All we have to do is remember to open the faucet and let it flow. This lesson was the dawn of a new day of thinking about money for me. Suddenly I understood that money was not *limited*, there was no definitive amount. It was as infinite and plentiful as water from the tap. It was up to me to regulate the flow. My job was to accept that money, like water, was always in full supply and, *depending on how much I felt I needed or believed I could handle*, that's how much I could release from the tap. What my mind thought determined my quota. The idea turned my world upside down. Instead of singing, "Get me to the church on time," I was singing "Get me to the tap, right now!"

Notice that I said: *money, like water, was always in full supply..., depending on how much I felt I needed or believed I could handle.* The statement means that all my supply of money, though potentially unlimited, was nevertheless dependant on my *consciousness* about it, and wrapped up in what I thought I deserved or was worthy of having. Intellectual comprehension of this spiritual understanding can be illusive. It's difficult to pin down; you have to work through it at both the *thinking* and the emotional levels. It can feel tenuous.

However, if we understand the invisible, all-powerful idea behind the spiritual concept of money we begin to comprehend the prospects in our Gold Mind.

Memorize this: for every material thing on earth, there is a spiritual equivalent that begins with an idea.

You may be feeling that this "thoughts are things" business is silly-talk and wondering why you bought *this* book in the first place. Let me respond. You bought this book because it rang a bell somewhere inside you. You were attracted, by a feeling, to the *thought* of what it might change in your life. At some level you wanted to improve your understanding and practices regarding money. If someone gave you this book it is because a bell rang in their head and connected you and your life with the information here. You (or your friend) were operating in the invisible world of emotions and ideas. You were attracted to the book, and so you bought it. Trust that impulse. If you have doubts about it now, give yourself some time. The chapter on Principles delves deeper into this world of the unseen and all will be illuminated. For now, just keep reading.

You don't just have to believe me, take it from the ever-abundant Reverend Ike who said,

> You are the manifestation of the ideas in your mind. The money that you have exactly matches the kind of ideas that you have in your mind. Ideas make millionaires. They also make multi-millionaires.

The spiritual aspect of Understanding in the Money Model is rooted in the ageless concept that the Universe Itself is the ultimate source of supply and that all of our individual and collective wealth/money/abundance/prosperity/wampum comes from this unlimited source and does not originate with any other person, place or thing. When we align our being and our thoughts with this endless and unlimited source of supply, we have mastered the square of Understanding.

Universal energy and supply are always everywhere present. There cannot be just a part of the whole present; the whole is always entirely present; like air. Since this Universal Whole contains everything, all the time, everywhere, it contains absolute wealth. If you have been wanting, praying for, increased wealth – what you need to know is that wealth, is absolutely present, and it is waiting for you to welcome it into your life.

> *If you think that people and things are your source, then people and things can cut you off. But if you know that God-in-you and only God-in-you is your Source of all good, then "they can't take that away from you." God-in-you may use many different people and things to deliver your good to you, but no person or thing is your source.*
>
> **-** Rev. Ike

One of the greatest lessons of The Money Model is that you must increase your understanding of what you deserve if you intend to have more, and you must perfect the methods you employ in order to handle what you *do* receive. The Money Model works on the tangible and intangible planes at the same time. They are inseparable. They feed each other.

Understand - get into your conscious awareness - that you live in an abundant source the same as a fish lives in water. It is your milieu.[2] It is available to you all the time, everywhere and it is deeper and more expansive than you could ever imagine. What you hold in your mind becomes more powerful when you also anchor it in your emotions.

Try this exercise to deepen your understanding:

> *Close your eyes and imagine yourself as a beautiful fish. Choose your colors and design your fabulous fins and tail the way you would have them. Now allow yourself to swim freely in abundant waters. Everywhere you look in each direction the water is unlimited. No matter how far you swim to the right, or to the left, there is plenty more. There is always more. Let yourself experience the feeling of being surrounded by the life-giving, invisible presence that sustains you and allows you the freedom to be completely who you are.*

[2] French word meaning *your surroundings.*

Swim around some more. Notice that you are not restricted. Nothing is holding you in one place, you have everything you need and you are enjoying a sense of total freedom. You are completely nurtured by your environment. If you have difficulty being a fish – imagine you are a bird moving through the unlimited sky. Substitute the image of water for air. Just get the point: you are in it, surrounded by it, completely supported by it. This is your milieu.

You may want to take a moment to write down your feelings about this exercise. It is critical that you understand this emotionally and that you create the awareness, inside yourself, of this unlimited source of supply.

Honor yourself. Make sure you have allowed the feeling of limitless plenty to soak in. Go back over the chapter and the exercise if you have any doubts. Proceed when you know for sure there is always enough of everything to go around.

When you have taken a moment to express your understanding, it is time to move onto the next Chapter: Values.

Tell me and I'll forget;
show me and I may remember;
involve me and I'll understand.
– Chinese Proverb

Chapter Six
Lesson 5:
The High Price of Value

It's not hard to make decisions
when you know what your values are.
– Roy Disney

Once we have achieved an understanding of something we consciously or subconsciously "rate it." We directly or indirectly assign it a value according to our own comparative system. **Value** is what society at large considers the rate of exchange to be and, more importantly, what you consider worthy of spending your time and money on.

Things only have the value that we give them.
– Moliere

Value causes you to make choices: This is better than *that*; I'll take *this* one, not *that* one; I'd like the shrimp instead of the steak. Or, I'll take both the surf and turf, *if* it's on the early bird special.

It doesn't matter whether you have inherited millions and your are reading this book looking to add meaning to your life, or if you are down to your last dime and trying to figure out what to do next. Integrating the concept of Value is your next step to financial empowerment. A multi-millionaire can be just as unhappy as a person fresh out of monetary resources. Conversely, they can both be just as happy, too.

There is no value in life except what you choose to
place upon it and no happiness in any place except
what you bring to it yourself.
– Henri David Thoreau

At some very deep level you already know everything you need to know about money and value. You possess it in your DNA. This book, this process, is simply a tool which allows you to stake your claim to the treasure you already have within. The key to the riches lives inside of you, even though you may not be aware of it all of the time. You know instinctively what works for you and what doesn't. You know what you like and what pleases you the most. You know where your inspiration comes from. You know what repels you. What you value is known at your depths. This is also where your gold lies.

Use this example: You may know that you prefer to spend time at the water rather than in the forest because of the feel of the grains of sand under your feet, the caress of the sea breeze against your skin, the whiff of salt dust in the air, the dance of the light upon the surface of the water, the whitecaps and the unseen power in the rhythm of the waves as they advance and retreat upon the shoreline. Somehow you sense comfort, safety, bonding and unity with the seashore. It is your place of choice because you are at one there with a presence greater than yourself and you connect with that presence at the primal level of your being.

Or maybe you prefer the grandeur of the redwoods: the tall majesty of trees, which are ancient and wise beyond your knowing, the keepers of mystic secrets of the ages and bearers of the blueprint of time within their core. Without the need for words the giants speak to your heart and your soul resounds with a grateful sense of returning home. You are wrapped in the comforting arms of the woodland and it is there you feel a sense of sacred belonging.

Perhaps "your place" is the endless ever-changing museum of a mountaintop, or a grotto, or a library or a temple. There are no right or wrong places. The place that has value to each of us, like everything else, is "ours" and is priceless to us.

No one teaches you how to feel good or how to prefer one place to the other. It comes to you naturally and instinctively. This is precisely how you learn to place value. What would you give to have the full experience of a moment like this? What would you exchange?

> *Happiness is that state of consciousness which proceeds from the achievement of one's values.*
> – Ayn Rand

Nearly everything in the world is free and, conversely, every thing has a price. I know it sounds like a contradiction in terms, but when you really stop to think about it, you know it's true. Air is free, but you'll pay a price for it if you scuba dive and want air to take with you on your underwater adventure. There are no parking meters on the waters of the ocean, but if you want to park your car and use a private beach, you'll pay a tariff for that privilege. What about the cost of bottled water? Water may be free and plentiful but we pay a price to haul it around in portable bottles.

Freedom has a price; and it is invaluable at the same time. Insuring freedom for one may cost millions of dollars or the life of another; one is measurable the other is valuable beyond measure. Sometimes you only learn to appreciate the value of a person, place or thing when it is taken away from you and you can no longer experience it.

Anything you lose automatically doubles in value.
– Mignon McLaughlin

Our four girl friends had very different ways of placing value in their lives. Sarah loved the glamorous life: being involved in gala events, hanging around with famous people, being seen in fancy restaurants. She found value in visiting places of note and associating with people of name. That excited her. She lived for it and would go to almost any extent and cost to sustain those pleasures. Her photography work brought her into the homes of the rich and famous; her social life revolved around the events and activities of celebrities; as such her attention was fixed on them most of the time. Being attached to this world put a spring in her step each morning and gave her a reason to exist. Stars who lit up the screen with their presence also illuminated her galaxy.

Marie loved being the belle of the ball and the life of the party. She also wanted to be seen as powerful and independently capable. She once drove herself to the hospital when she had appendicitis, not wanting to trouble anyone else. But Marie lived moment-to-moment and dollar-to-dollar. She did not value having a savings account if it got in the way of the movie last night, the dress today, or the fun-whatever-the-adventure-tomorrow. She's was all for it, raring to go and primed to head out the door on a moment's notice. Like all the women, Marie had bills to pay, but she couldn't be bothered with some company's calendar, so she paid her bills when she had the money. The rest of the time, she just didn't answer the phone. Don't misunderstand, Marie worked very hard, was extremely generous and would be at your home in the middle of the night if you needed her. She was also extremely creative; she just couldn't hold onto money. It was too slippery for her. She'd rather be out having fun or creating a memory. *"Woo hoo!"* And who's to say she's wrong? She isn't financially secure, but she's a heck of a party guest.

Angela loved travel more than anything else in the world. Well, except maybe sex. She liked that too. Put them together and she had a home run. Angela had a lot of boyfriends, sometimes several simultaneously but never without their individual consent and knowledge. A couple of the boyfriends would even take her on lovely trips once or twice a year. For decades this was her pattern: serial relationships (and multiple trips) until she met the man of her dreams. Now she's completely happy. They both travel, usually independently. Seldom in the same place at the same time, they only see each other a few weeks at a time maybe three or four times a year. The rest of the time, they are traveling, separately. The relationship works for them. The first few days home from their respective trips, they show each other snapshots and catch up. After that, they enjoy a couple of weeks of romance, walks on the beach and sunset suppers. Time flies and eventually it's time to pack up and head off to another part of the world. It's *"Bye-bye Sweetie"* and off they go again.

Angela is not a jet-setter, she travels conservatively. She seldom pays more than $24 a night for a room and chooses to ride the local transportation. She is astonishingly well-traveled, fearless, and has been to distant places where only the military has been allowed: the military and *Angela.* Her photographs take your breath away and she has met some of the most interesting and beautiful people on earth. She has a world filled with friends and if we had a contest, I'll bet we'd be hard-pressed to come up with the name of a town she hasn't been to.

Although most of her travel is for her own edification, Angela had the dream to spend a month in a birthing hospital in Africa. She saved her money for three years to earn the airfare and expenses. Her time there was spent helping women bare children in the middle of a desert. Her kindness helped so many through the ordeal of labor. To her this opportunity was invaluable and she willingly paid about $10,000 from her own savings for the privilege.

> *The value of life is not in the length of days, but in the use we make of them; a man may live long yet very little.*
> – Michel de Montaigne

Zelda, on the other hand, does not enjoy roughing it. She is not a camper. She would rather watch a documentary about an exotic and primitive region than encounter the bugs, dust and ox carts. Zelda has traveled around the world and enjoyed many different cultures. She also appreciates a comfortable room, clean linens and identifiable cuisine.

Zelda values a well-organized trip with an ample amount of leisure time to enjoy the locale and become immersed in the culture. She would rather spend four or five days in one exciting city than hop a tourist-laden bus and cover four metropoli in three days. Zelda prefers quality to quantity and wants time to explore the local flea markets *and* jewelry shops.

Each of the friends has a different set of values. Angela would prefer to take three inexpensive trips to Zelda's single expensive one. Marie would love to go on a trip, but she might not be able to come up with the airfare or the hotel expenses. (But she would *absolutely love* to go.) When Sarah travels she wants to take a celebrity with her, or meet up with one along the way. And name restaurants would have to be part of the itinerary even though the cost of a glass of wine would feed an entire family in Angela's neck of the woods.

> *There is no such thing as absolute value in this world. You can only estimate what a thing is worth to you.*
> – Charles Dudley Warner

Each woman is, of course, absolutely entitled to her own values. Each of them can and does run her life the way she wants. You'd have to ask each of them if they were happy. I can tell you for sure and without a doubt that Zelda is.

Now the focus turns to you. Are you happy? What would make you happier? What do you value most? Before we move on, let's do a little mental exercise to stir your imagination and uncover some of the hidden values that may be affecting your financial situation and your happiness. Remember, we are looking to uncover any hidden treasure that might be lurking under the surface of your conscious thought. Play along and let's see what you discover.

Close your eyes; relax into a steady breathing rhythm. Allow yourself to respond emotionally to the words as they enter your mind. Respond with the first impression that you feel.

> *Surprise visit*
> *Winning ticket*
> *Family reunion*
> *Holiday celebration*
> *Game show*
> *Bubble bath*
> *Commerce*
> *Honesty*
> *Favorite dish*
> *Good job*
> *Paid vacation*
> *Compliment*
> *Best friend*
> *Love*
> *Hospital*
> *Windfall*
> *Aching back*
> *Unemployment*
> *Nature*
> *Special Delivery*
> *Kind word*
> *Violent storm*
> *Unhappy child*
> *Moment of Victory*
> *Favorite song*
> *Price*
> *Compassion*
> *Dream*
> *When my ship comes in*
> *Unlimited*
> *Emotional experience*
> *Happiness*
> *Legacy*

When we speak about value we want to consider both material and non-material qualities. As you may have noticed, the word association list moved back and forth between the two worlds. You were asked to consider visible and tangible concepts as well as emotional and intangible ones. Your responses indicated the thoughts you have about, and the values you place on, those images. What did you learn about yourself? Was there anything that surprised you?

If you have clearly defined and well-established values your life is strongly guided by what you hold dear and make important. We discussed the source of those values in earlier chapters. If you just wander through life or go too far afield you may wake up one day to find that you are lost in a sea of indecision. You could even drown there if you are not wearing a life jacket.

> *I conceive that the great part of the miseries of mankind are brought on by the false estimates they have of the value of things.*
> – Benjamin Franklin

At this stage it is imperative that you become consciously aware of your own values. British journalist Alex Hamilton said, "Those who stand for nothing fall for anything." Haven't we all done that to an extent? Haven't we all had the wool pulled over our eyes?

The search for meaning and the establishment of values goes far beyond the common prankster. Values give voice to your soul. Your life has dimension when you live it from a core of values that you create, adhere to, and celebrate.

When you are willing to bring your values out into the open you are able to fully comprehend the base you are working from. By understanding the base you operate from you can begin to make the positive changes which lead you to wealth.

Here is an exercise to assist you in recognizing the core concepts that you, consciously or unconsciously, hold to be of value.

Step # 1: Discovering Your Inner Values

On a separate piece of paper make a list of everything you value. I offer here a few suggestions to get your mind working.

Money	Job	Home	Family
Parents	Children	Siblings	Community
Health	Creativity	Possessions	Self-Esteem
Friends	Religion	Sex	Activity
Politics	Satisfaction	Truth	Global Awareness
Compassion	Honesty	Integrity	Education
Reliability	Hard work	Commitment	Security
Service	Principles	Wisdom	Location
Loyalty	Prestige	Awards	Accomplishment
Power	Accolades	Intelligence	Independence
Attraction	Partnership	Unity	Openness

Write a full sentence after each word. Example: *Education* is important to me because it gives me the freedom to choose how I earn a living. Be sure to take the time to indulge and define your feelings about each word you use. Feel free to add or delete words you don't connect to from this initial list.

Step # 2: Understanding and Clarification

a)   Take your list, no matter how long it is and mark off your Top Ten Values by putting a "T" next to them.

b)   Do the same thing for your Bottom Ten and put a "B" next to them.

c)   Next, from the "T's" pick your Top Five values and from the "B's" pick your bottom five values. (The Bottom Five are those values you would be willing to give up. The Top Five are those values that are essential to you.)

d)   Compare your Top Five values with what you *actually* spend your time on. (Does reviewing your Bottom Five give you any clues?)

This exercise helps you identify, clarify, sort and file what you value. Where you spend your time is an indicator of what you value. After completing this exercise, you should have a fairly accurate picture of what you consider to be of value and,

42

perhaps more importantly, whether or not that is where you want to be focusing your time and energy. The next step is to put your values into action so your life becomes aligned with your desires. You can think of them as a chiropractic adjustment for your invisible backbone. We all can use some alignment from time to time, can't we?

The next exercise can be done repeatedly any time you feel the need for adjustment.

Step #3: Living in Power

Complete the following sentences using your Top Five Values as your guide.

I want _____

I have_____

I need_____

I enjoy_____

I desire_____

I understand_____

I appreciate _____

I'm happy_____

I want to_____

I always_____

I believe_____

I will trade_____

I seldom_____

I choose_____

I'm willing_____

It pleases_____

I must_____

I respect_____

My money mentor(s) is/are_____

My money mentor taught me (I learned from my mentor)
_____

I am convinced_____
_____

I am ready to_____
_____

Do yourself a favor and take as long as you need for this exercise. One more time, review your Bottom Five values and honestly observe whether you might be spending too much time or energy, or both, on those values which you have tagged as non-essential. Review your statements and see how they align with your Top Ten Values. You'll never hang on to your gold unless your ducks are lined up.

The inner work you are doing is great. No matter your age or situation, clarification of your money thinking will benefit you tremendously. When you are secure about your values and the place they have in your life, move on to the next area of our Money Model. You will need to bring along your list of Top Ten values, as they are the skeleton for the body of Principles we will encounter next.

Should you choose not to do these exercises, know that you will miss the depth of change that this book can provide. Take the time, and honor yourself enough, to use these processes to dig for your gold. Without the work, the time spent prospecting, there can be no reward.

Nowadays people know the price of everything
and the value of nothing.
– Oscar Wilde

Chapter Seven
Lesson 6:
Principles

Life does not consist mainly, or even largely, of facts and happenings. It consists mainly of the stream of thought (energy) that is forever flowing through one's head.
– Mark Twain

Most of us get a chill when we hear the word Principle. It reminds us of being sent to a formidable disciplinarian in a stuffy wood paneled office who rakes us over the coals for our unacceptable, in their opinion, behavior. (What do you mean you never got sent to the principal? I was there at least twice a week!) The Principles we're talking about in this book are definitely not that, they are beneficent. They us offer solid, constant and helpful grace. The more you know and understand about Principles, the greater control you will have over your life and your finances. And, the more you will be able to put them to use for creating your affluent life; which is the whole point of this book.

Principles are a set of non-discriminatory invisible laws that always remain the same. They are everlasting and neutral. Principles have worked the same way for as long as the Universe has been in existence, and they will continue to operate powerfully and anonymously for the rest of time. They can neither be created nor destroyed, they just are. There is something quite comforting in the realization of these unseen powers.

As "dry" as it may appear at first, learning about Principles can actually be interesting and enlightening. In Chapter Eight we'll discuss more about how and why they work; for now, let's explore what they are, why we require them, and how we can use them to increase our prosperity.

In his book *The 7 Habits of Highly Effective People,* Steven Covey defines Principles as "...deep fundamental truths, classic truths, generic common denominators... tightly interwoven threads running with exactness, consistency, beauty, and strength through the fabric of life".

Nature has principles. The natural law of gravity pulls things to the center of the earth which, requires that: What goes up, comes down. It is a Principle. It does not matter if a man, woman or camel tosses an item into the air; it comes down the same way, and at the same velocity regardless of who or what tossed it into the air. Rain is another natural, neutral, force. Rain occurs when certain elements in nature are united. It takes water, warm air and gravity to produce rain. Then, it rains with equal intensity on the rich and the poor alike. The sun shines without prejudice on people of all sizes, shapes and colors, and on all things, in the identical way. Rain is as wet on me as it is on the Queen of England. We learn about the workings of these Universal truths and laws every day. We validate our understanding of them through the personal experience of our lives.

> *Principles always have natural consequences attached to them. There are positive consequences when we live in harmony with the principle. There are negative consequences when we ignore them. The more we know of correct principles, the greater is our personal freedom to act wisely.*
> – Steven Covey

It is widely held that the more you know about Principles, the wiser your actions become because Principles are absolutely non-negotiable. You can't outsmart them. You can't cheat them; they will always operate according to their own law and the invisible mandates they follow.

So, why are they of any concern to you? What should you do with them? The first thing you want to do is to understand and embrace what is going on in the invisible realm. The second thing is to figure out how to use the Principles to your own advantage. Let me give you an example of how financial principles work in real life.

Principles/Law in Action

My mother and father lived in the Northwest most of their married lives. They built their own home by hand,[1] just as my grandfather and grandmother had done. When they retired they wanted to live summers in the Northwest and winters in

---

[1] See Chapter Fifteen for further details

California. They found a nice house near Temecula and bought it directly from the builder. It was the first time my mother had been able to decorate a home from scratch and have it exactly as she wanted.

I remember how excited she was to have the home decorator consultant come over and show her fabric swatches. She decorated one room in warm Santa Fe blush tones, another room in deeper blues and purples. She chose traditional pastel tapestry for the living room and she bought all new furniture in a contemporary whitewashed stain. Her curtains and shades were bright, new and fresh. She was extremely happy in her California home surrounded by all the newness and beauty of her own creating.

My father passed on in 1993. He left a living trust for my mother to live on which provided amply for her life and for her care, should she require it. My mother joined my father in 2001 and I inherited her home with all of her personal touches. Once I had donated or distributed most her personal items, I put the house on the market. Because I lived 100 miles away from Temecula, I wanted an agent who was going to take good care of the house and handle it with care and respect.

To honor my mother, who loved the house so much, and who had dedicated so much loving energy attending to its every detail, I wanted it to be shown, sold and embraced just as she left it. Her imprint was embedded in every room and it was beautiful. The inside was warm and it felt like you could walk in, sit down, pour a glass of lemonade, watch TV, and feel right at home. Furniture and all, I decided that this would be the perfect way to sell the house. I set a price (for discussion, let's call it $300,000) and interviewed ten agents before choosing one to list with.

The first agent told me I was *out of my mind* and I needed to move all of the furniture out right away and choose a realistic price of $200,000 for a fast sale. He said there were estate sales companies locally and I should just let them sell the "junk." He and his co-worker may have been impeccably dressed, and carried current high-end electronics, but they clearly did not share my concerns or intentions.

The second agent wanted to conduct open houses every Tuesday, Saturday and Sunday for anyone who happened to drop in. I wanted people to make an appointment to see the house once they had been pre-qualified to purchase it. I didn't want non-essential traffic wandering through the house soiling Mother's carpets. Another agent suggested we *auction* the house and furnishings off to the highest bidder! I could hear, my mother's mother spinning in her grave at the very thought of it!

Finally, I found the perfect agent. She was a young, smiling and vibrant woman who understood exactly what I wanted to do. She was a successful agent who was willing to completely support me on every issue. She said, *"Why not!"* to every idea I had. She was exactly who I was looking for. She shared my vision. She completely accepted my reasons and my intentions. The only thing she said was that it might take a little while to find the perfect buyer, but find him or her we would. All showings were to be by appointment only. We listed the house at the price I *knew* it was worth. We listed it furnished; down to the area rugs and flower arrangements.

There were those who told me I was setting myself up for failure. Others who said the house would never sell at that price, especially with the furniture. I held out. I just knew this was the perfect course of action to take. It wasn't necessarily easy. There were gardens to maintain, weeds to be pulled, taxes to be paid, cleaning and maintenance to be handled and multiple freeway intense trips to oversee the property. I held steadfast to my vision.

It took six months, but the perfect buyer appeared. In fact, this house, exactly as it was, turned out to be the answer to the buyers' prayers. They were from the Mid-west but needed a home out-west to be close to their ailing mother. They didn't think they'd ever find a home that was furnished. They didn't think they'd ever find a home as perfect in size for them as this was. They never expected it would also come with a TV, a stereo, outdoor furniture and flower arrangements. They were thrilled. They loved every detail. They didn't balk at the price. They happily paid it and even ended up buying the truck that was parked in the garage.

Their desire for acquiring a home was as clear and perfect as my intention for selling it. Because each of us was motivated by pure good the invisible law of attraction connected us. It was as if we each had radar for the other. There it was, the perfect solution for both parties. The deal was completed in three short weeks. The agreement was smooth and the buyers even sent me a thank you note on one of my mother's note cards that they found fallen behind a shelf in the garage.

Do you think this was sheer luck, or might there have been something more happening? It may have looked like "luck" or "happenstance" but I am here to tell you, it wasn't. When I assess this particular series of intention, action and result, I believe it can be reduced to a few points that, practiced over and over, will unfailingly deliver results. Let me share with you what I know and how I used these principles to accomplish exactly what I set out to accomplish.

It begins with a core belief: *Thoughts are Things* and our thoughts are powerful.

This truth is not new, it has been taught since the time of the ancient Greek and Roman philosophers. It has been reiterated by master teachers from Benjamin Franklin to Dale Carnegie, Napoleon Hill, Stephen Covey, Terry Cole-Whittaker, Marianne Williamson and many more. When we really grasp this concept, we change our lives instantly.

Do you want to experiment a little? Go ahead and try this exercise.

> *Close your eyes for just a moment and recall an incident or an experience that was not particularly pleasant. Recall a time when someone may have acted harshly towards you, or lashed out inappropriately. Bring into your mind a memory of that moment. Notice how you feel. Notice what is happening in your body. What are your hands doing? How does your stomach feel? What is the state of your neck and shoulders? Really take notice of what is going on in your body. What are you tasting?*

Now, re-imagine the incident. Cut the person some slack. Decide that they just received some terrible news. Decide that they have a migraine headache. Decide that they are in more need of compassion and understanding than you are. It may be a stretch, but try it anyway. Let them off the hook for a moment. Un-accuse them. Excuse them. Forgive them. If you can, even go a step further and see them as a beautiful being. Picture the experience being a positive one. Perhaps there was a revelation in this for you. Perhaps there was a hidden gift. Perhaps a misunderstanding occurred that, given a new light, looks differently. Once you have turned the tables on this incident, check in with your body and see how it feels now. Compare how you are feeling now to what you were feeling earlier in this exercise. How are you? What are your hands doing now? How about your insides, your neck and shoulders?

A question: Did you just read the exercise, or did you really take the time to consciously do it? Nothing in your life will change if you don't work this process and do the lessons! If you did the exercise, do you feel any different? Have you experienced how powerful your thoughts are? Simply by shifting your mind from a negative to a positive you created a different experience in your body. Principles are validated in our own lives by our experience. To believe in them fully is to actually feel their power at work.

Like gravity, all Principles are here to help us. Take *The Law (Principle) of Attraction* as an example. Much has been written about it lately and certainly "The Secret" portrayed it actively and effectively in the DVD, and the movie "What the Bleep Do We Know" did the same. The Principle is simply this: Like Attracts Like. And since the mind itself does not distinguish between real or imaginary[2], you can in fact attract something to your life by thinking it so.

So why isn't everybody rich, then? Don't we all think we want to be? Why is there starvation in the world, and war? Because

---

[2] Experimental psychologists have proven that the human nervous system cannot tell the difference between an "actual" experience and the experience imagined in detail. University of Chicago.

this vital principle is not properly understood. For the "Law of Attraction" – which is actually the Principle of Cause and Effect in action – to work effectively to create your desires these three things have to be present.

1) Unfaltering Belief: You must completely believe and understand that this Law is powerful and works. You must also believe in the power of your thoughts to create what you want using this Law. In other words, you must believe you deserve it, you must believe it will be accomplished, and you must believe the thoughts you hold in your mind can make it so.

2) Intense Focus: You must focus clearly and with *specific* detail on what you want. You must see the outcome as real and experience it as having happened. You must be able to project yourself into the future so that you can actually see it done, feel the results and experience what it's like to have attained your desire and be living in the results.

3) Seal with Zeal: You must seal your vision by the power of your feelings, so the vision becomes an integrated part of your emotional body. You must find your inner source of intense fire and passion and crank up the heat. You must stick it in the oven and "cook it," emotionally speaking. You are required to turn the heat up to about nine hundred degrees and fortify the form with the force of your internal fire.

Step Three is where failure most often occurs. People forget that completion is in the firing. You must first believe it, then you must state it clearly and begin to experience it , then you absolutely must fuel the vision with your passion and desire for it. And I mean you've got to *feel* the burn. Your mind must be the blowtorch of conviction for this to take effect.

> Truly, "thoughts are things" and powerful things at that, when they are mixed with definiteness of purpose, persistence, and a burning desire for their translation into riches, or other material objects.
> – Napoleon Hill

When was the last time you had the feeling of "fire in the belly?" When was the last time you felt "stoked" and full of fire? That's the feeling you must rekindle, at the physical passionate level to conclude this process.

Once you've done that, you can let it go and let it become. The Universe has heard your call and is already on the job. Your vision, having been clearly stated and cooked *will* occur. Just leave it alone. As Paul McCartney says, "Let it Be." Go on about your business, unless you've asked for something like having a child; then you better get going, clean out those old closets and prepare the nursery. If you have done all three steps correctly; whatever it is *will* happen for you.

Remember, the Universe retains the vibrational[3] pattern of the thought only when emotion/passion fires it. Think of this process as if you were casting pottery. You must first *believe* that a cold, wet lump of clay can be turned into a work of art. The next thing you do is *focus* by making it into the shape you want. Then you *fire* it. If you don't fire it in the kiln with intense heat the shape will not remain. To fire the pottery is to "cook" the intention and the vision into something real. Once your vision has been seared and sealed it becomes something tangible. You can *feel* the power of it.

What happens so often is that a person is only half convinced this can really work. Or, they've been exposed to a complicated system with a lot of steps and a theme song. It's lame. There is no force, there is no power, there is only a doubtful presence creating a limp and listless want, a recipe for failure. Please understand, the Principle of Cause and Effect will respond to lameness. You put out lame; you get back lame. If you put out powerful thoughts; you receive powerful results. That's the Law in action. When there is no power behind the thinking there can be no potent reciprocation. There must be a powerful Cause before there can be a powerful Effect.

The three steps may seem like a difficult ladder to climb if you've had no practice and think you've experienced no victories. But look at the last time you got results you set out

---

[3] The term "vibrational" here refers to the Quantum Physics theory that all matter is composed of light waves, sound waves or vibrational patterns in the smallest sub-atomic particle. The movement of the atoms of creation result in vibrations that can be seen felt and measured.

to get. It doesn't matter how big or small. Break down the parts to it and see if they match up to the three steps described in this book. If they do, and they will, then you're on the right track and you may just need a little help with refinement of your skills. We all have this power to create real things from the gold within our minds.

Take the challenge. Find something in your life that is working well and analyze it. See if you can locate the *belief* you had, see if you can determine what you *focused* on and then recall how you were able to *fire up* that belief and feel it intensely in your emotional body. What happened in your life when all three elements were present?

The last step is the invisible key. You must bring your vision into connection with your emotions. You've got to stir the power of conviction. You've got to feel the intensity and the burn. Principles always respond. It's up to you to put them to use.

When it comes to money and finances, the Principles in The Money Model apply flawlessly every time. Go over it again it if you need to. Don't *la dee dah* over this information if you are serious about creating and maintaining wealth.

Before we continue onto Acquisition, I want to introduce you to the **Six Timeless Truths About Money** and wealth building, so you can begin to apply the Principles to them.

Once you understand the Six Truths in the next chapter we move to the *Acquisition* of wealth and divulge more mental techniques for creating your prosperity.

On matters of style, swim with the current,
on matters of Principle stand like a rock.
– Thomas Jefferson

Chapter Eight
Lesson 7:
The Six Timeless Truths about Money

In order to know more, do more, and be more
we must have more; we must have things to use,
for we learn, and do, and become, only by using things.
We must get rich, so that we can live more.
– Wallace D. Wattles

Money is a subject packed with emotional history. Whether you realize it or not, you *have* a unique relationship with money and most of us have placed some type of value judgment on that relationship. I am asking you to put all of those considerations, emotional ties and judgments aside for the moment. Wipe the slate clean. Start over. As far as money is concerned, forget what you thought you knew. Today new thoughts are coming alive!

The next six statements you read are all you need to incorporate new *money thinking* into your life. These Six Timeless Truths compose the foundation for prospecting the, as yet undiscovered, wealth and prosperity that lies within you. Give the boot to any other thoughts except these six and you'll be well on your way to mining that gold.

1) No person place or thing is your source of money or prosperity. The Universe holds an open door to all who have the courage and the mind-set to ask for and receive their abundance.

2) Money exists both in the visible and the invisible world. It is a concept, an idea, a thought, as well as a currency of the physical exchange of goods and services.

3) The supply of money you have in your life is only limited by your thinking. What's in your wallet is ruled by what's in your mind. There is a physical equivalent for every mental thought. (A mental cause behind every physical effect.)

4) You have every right to share in the riches of this world. The Universe is your ally because it can express itself more fully through you when you accept its abundance. When you

achieve wealth the Universe has succeeded in its job of providing unconditional supply.

5) Fear is the only barrier to our prosperity. The lack of prosperity is tied far more to what we fear than to what we deserve.

6) The Laws governing money do not discriminate against any person, place or thing. They operate identically for the Honest John and the criminal alike. These money Laws are in effect 24 hours a day, 365 days a year and one more day for leap year. Like Las Vegas, the Principles/Truths/Laws never close, not even on holidays. (The Laws of the invisible and the visible worlds are coming up after this next exercise.)

These six points sum up *everything* you need to believe about money in order to have affluence in your life.[1]

Before continuing with your reading take a moment to reflect on *your* thoughts about money as they relate to the six points you have just read.

> *Sit back, close your eyes and relax. Take a few deep breaths. When you've been able to clear your mind and create a blank slate, open your eyes and answer the following questions.*
>
> *In the past I considered _____*
> *to be the source of my money.*
> *Today I know universal supply is unlimited and my money comes from this inexhaustible resource.*
>
> *In the past I believed money was _____*
> *_____*
> *Today I know money is a symbol of continuous increase and is the means through which prosperity is exchanged.*
>
> *In the past I have believed _____*
> *_____*
> *Today I desire a larger life so that I may become the full expression of the universe acting though me as abundance.*

1. Author's promise.

In the past I have believed my right to wealth was
_____

Today I believe there is potential affluence seeking to express itself more fully in my life. I need only to claim it and continue its increase in order to attain it.

In the past I was afraid money _____
_____

Today I replace any negative thoughts about money with my belief in the bounty of creation. I possess all of the talents and everything else I need to attract and manage the unlimited bounty of the Universe.

In the past I thought I_____
_____

Today I believe having wealth and living prosperously is available to everyone. I choose affluence and the fulfillment of nature as my companion

Use these seven powerful statements to correct any thinking you may have that is not in agreement with the Six Timeless Truths About Money. Review the "today" statements until they are solidified as your core beliefs. When you accomplish the switch you will witness the Laws of the invisible world (on the following pages) falling into action to create prosperity in your life.

Perhaps you are already familiar with the visible and the invisible laws and principles that govern your world. These Laws constitute the foundation from which the Six Timeless Truths About Money spring. The amazing truth is that you were born with the soul knowledge of all of these Universal truths at the core of your soul. They are already firmly imbedded in your DNA.

The next few pages may just be a refresher course for what your inner self has always known. If this information is new to you, read it with care.

This body of knowledge constitutes the intangible blueprint to your abundance. Once you understand the foregoing, you'll be ready to start mining your treasure.

The Laws of the Invisible World:

1) Law of Unity/ One

There is only one essence/energy/power/source/intelligence that unites all of creation. It has never been more aptly put than by Carl Sagan who said, "We are all star stuff." Every particle of the Universe is contained in every other piece and linked by the Grand Poobah of Divine Intelligence. Everyone and every thing is connected to, and by, this Universal Intelligence. We can't escape it, we can't deny it, we can't erase it, but if we're smart we'll use it. It's as reasonable and uncomplicated as harnessing electricity, and far less difficult than herding cats.

> *Whatever substance is at all, the whole of substance must be; and because substance is omnipresent, the whole of universal substance must be present in space at the same time.*
> *– Eric Butterworth*

2) Law of Becoming

This law refers to the subtle changes of growth and transformation in each particle of the cosmos. Everything is always changing; nothing remains the same; it is always becoming that which it is to be next. An infant becomes a child, grows into a teenager, then matures to an adult. We do not see *becoming* as it comes; we only recognize it when it has occurred. This law means that what was yesterday, is not the same today, nor will it be the same tomorrow. It reminds us to remain open; to live in life's flow, going with the current of the stream of life and not against it. Hanging onto the past only causes us extreme grief and impedes our personal progress and growth.

> *Life is a process of becoming, a combination of states we have to go through. Where people fail is that they wish to elect a state and remain in it. This is a kind of death.*
> *– Anais Nin*

3) Law of Evolution

This Law guarantees that our becoming and unfolding is always in the direction of *good*. The natural path of life, existence, and experience progresses towards new levels of goodness. Each step in our life expands our consciousness and improves the quality of our soul. It is our acceptance of this truth which allows us to see and feel the good in all that occurs. The good may be disguised as a set back, an accident or even a tragic event, but at its very core the Law of Evolution says that everything is ultimately *good*.

> *Rest assured that in whatever station of life we are placed, princely or lowly, it contains the lessons and experiences necessary at the moment for our evolution, and gives us the best advantage for the development of ourselves.*
> – Edward Bach

All of our experiences are valuable. If we are wise, we are willing to learn from each moment, as though it were a Divine Gift, chosen and wrapped just for us, and given with love so that we may grow and prosper because of it.

4) Law of Morality

The human conscience is the inner container of timeless wisdom. In the highest state we all are equal, all diverse and all riches and graces are to be shared by everyone, unilaterally. We were born with these inherent rights and blessings. Everyone has a sense of right action inside of them. In spite of those who would legislate it, morality cannot be mandated; it must be summoned from the secret core of our individual souls. We discover morality in the wonder of our own nature, in the compassion of one another, and in the very celebration of life itself.

> *Reverence for life affords me my fundamental principles of morality.*
> – Albert Schweitzer

5) Law of Abundance.

The Universe is composed of energy which continually renews itself. In this Universe there is plenty. There is abundance. The spirit of the Universe is generous and it will always give you what you need in order to complete your journey. In the spiritual world there can't be anything but enough. What can be thought in the mind can be manifested on the earth.

Abundance is almost boring in its repetition. It has cycles, rhythm, and pulse. It can be activated, stimulated, primed and enhanced. It cannot be stopped, contained or destroyed. Abundance is in every particle of nature: the oceans, the stars, the sky, the air; it is everything we can conceive of and a whole lot more. There is no lack in the Universe. There is however, a human-designed flimsy and sloppy system for distribution. The Law of Abundance cannot and does not discriminate against anyone for any reason; people do.

> *Cats seem to go on the principle that it never does any harm to ask for what you want.*
> – Joseph Wood Krutch

We've just covered the Laws of the invisible world. How many of these ideas were new to you? How many had you simply overlooked, or forgotten, or forgotten to apply to your beliefs about being abundant? Did insights result from your reading? The next set of Laws operate from the core of the invisible world; you can see the material proof of the invisible Laws in action when you digest this next group.

Laws of the Visible world:

> *The physical laws of the Universe are actually this whole process of divinity in motion, or consciousness in motion. When we understand these laws and apply them in our lives, anything we want can be created, because the same laws that nature uses to create a forest, or a galaxy, or a star, or a human body can also bring about the fulfillment of our deepest desires.*
> – Deepak Chopra
> *The Seven Spiritual Laws of Success*

1) The Law of Cause & Effect

This principle is also commonly known as the Law of Karma, or the Boomerang Law. What you put out comes back to you - multiplied. Awareness of this Law originated in Babylonian times but can be found in the postulates of Galileo[1]: For every action there is an equal and opposite reaction. You can use this law to bring money, affluence and an endless flow of good things to you.

> *Nothing can come to you unless you believe you deserve it, and nothing can go from you unless you believe you don't deserve it.*
>
> – Rev. Ike

2) The Law of Attraction

Coming on the heels of The Law of Cause & Effect is The Law of Attraction. It ensures that all conditions and situations will be attracted to you so you will be able to eventually master your life goals and complete your purpose. The Law of Attraction works by reacting to your thoughts to summon the experiences you need for growth, development and enrichment. The catch phrase "We create our own reality," simply means your mind chooses whether you see a circumstance in a positive or a negative light. Your circumstances are the proof of the expression of your thoughts.

> *There is an innate drive in living matter to perfect itself.*
>
> – Albert Szent-Gyorgyi
> Nobel Prize winning Biologist

3) The Law of Correspondence

Your outer world is a reflection of what you are on the inside. In some cases, the outer world is a mask for the inner world. One may attempt to cover up what may be lacking inside with external decoration; but eventually the truth emerges. The real way to change your exterior world is through work on the internal, not vice versa. Your inner world thrives on a banquet

---

[1] If you thought the idea was one of Newton's Theories, please note that Newton credits Galileo with the discovery of this, the first theory.

of positive thoughts, positive affirmations, non-judgmental conversations and encouragement in order to create prosperity. If you take care to choose wisely what you put into your mind it will return to your life substance and experience of equal quality. It has been said of computers, "Garbage in: garbage out." This truth also applies to your mind.

> *Truth is exact correspondence with reality.*
> – Paramahansa Yogananda

4) Law of Polarity

True unity requires the presence of diversity. The whole is made of its individual parts and no amount of force can make the diverse parts fit together except through the energy field of compatibility. Everything in nature has a positive or a negative charge and is always operating in relationship to something else. The natural order is to create a balance between all opposing forces. Nothing in the Universe happens by chance. Always present at the heart of all life is order and balance. True wealth is a product of authentic balance.

> *Without contraries there is no progression.*
> *Attraction and repulsion, reason and energy, love*
> *and hate, are necessary to human existence.*
> – William Blake

5) Law of Grace

Grace, simply put, is the opposite of interference. In Grace all thought and all actions are motivated by purest intention. The Law of Grace *allows* everything to be what it is, and supports it in being true to itself. You are allowed and supported to be exactly as you are. However, the Law also requires that you allow *others* to be as they are. Gratitude for, and connection with, every living thing is implied. If you can love people and things outside of yourself for their intrinsic untouched beauty, you have fulfilled this Law. Grace is essential to prosperity.

> *Grace has been defined as the outward*
> *expression of the inward harmony of the soul.*
> – William Hazlitt

6) Law of Release

In order to acquire something in either the physical or invisible world, you must release your attachment to having it. Whatever you want, you must let go. On the surface this seems to be a paradox; why wouldn't you hang on to that which you cherished?

Fresh air cannot flow into a closed room. The windows and doors must be wide open for new air to enter and freshen. This law does not require you to say "good bye" to everyone in your life or to throw all of your possessions away; it only asks that you allow yourself to appreciate your divine perfection just as you are. When you are able to embody this truth you will have more than you need. As bizarre as it may sound, the more you make friends with the concept of release, the more you attract into your life.

> *Let your imagination release your imprisoned possibilities.*
> – Robert H. Schuller

7) The Law of 51%

There is one last Law. When I learned it, it gilded all my results and gave me renewed faith in all that I believed. It super-charged the entire process for me. The secret is simple but powerful: All you have to do is be 51% convinced of your thought/vision/intention for it to come to fruition. There is room for you to have a little human skepticism, but your clarity and your conviction must be over the 50% mark. You must be at 51% or above. There's nothing preventing you from being at 100%, of course, but if you find yourself somewhat short of the mark, that's okay. Just make sure you're 1% over the 50% line and you will score. (Pay close attention to the story about my father in Chapter Ten.)

There is a lot to think about here. Let me summarize these concepts as they apply to you and your life:

- All spiritual laws and principles regarding money are contained within the Laws we have just considered.
- You are unified with, and in, all of Creation.

- Just as Creation is always in flux, you are also changing and becoming renewed every day.
- You are evolving and headed in the direction of fulfillment and you have embedded within you the timeless wisdom of right action.
- There are no limits in this opulent Universe; you are welcome to it *all*.
- What you give attention to, you attract.
- Your outer world is a mirror of your inner thought.
- You are one of many individualized parts of the whole, and you are perfect and perfectly supported exactly as you are.
- The charge is to allow that the same truths are true for all other beings in creation.
- Even though it may appear a paradox, the more you are willing to release a person or thing; the faster it will return to you, increased.
- 51% is the magic number for success and ownership in all matters.

Read and re-read these principles until you fully understand them at the very core of your being. It is interesting to note that, each Law finds agreement with every major religion and teaching in this world. Ernest Holmes said that at the core of every philosophy is a golden thread that weaves truth through its doctrine. Even those who would fight over beliefs need only research further into their own spirituality to find the common thread among us all.

Once you befriend these Laws and integrate them, allowing them to become your core beliefs, you will automatically change the way you think and operate in the world. As a direct result of that change, your abundance will unfold as easily as the rosebud opens when it is encouraged by the summer sun.

Understand these Laws, operate within them according to Principle and your acquisition of money contained in the next chapter will be a breeze.

It is not impossibilities, which fill us with the deepest despair; but possibilities, which we have failed to realize.
– Robert Mallett

Chapter Nine
Lesson 8:
Acquisition

Fortunate indeed, is the man who takes exactly the right measure of himself, and holds a just balance between what he can acquire and what he can use.
– Peter Mere Latham

Acquisition means the way money comes into your life and the channels through which you attain your money. It is rooted in the spirit of acquiring money.

The way in which we acquire money is just as important as the acquisition itself. When we are aligned with our true purpose, money flows to us with invisible grace. If we are at odds with our purpose, or we are feeling stifled, forced or oppressed, the money that flows into our lives is linked to discord; and our relationship with it will be chaotic.

This is true because money by itself is neutral. A dollar bill is a dollar bill: a piece of government printed paper that doesn't care into whose hands it falls. It is this invisible neutrality that produces the greatest impact on our lives and fortunes.

For protection some banks often mark bills with imperceptible powder that can be detected by specialized equipment. Other banks mark money with dye packs that burst in the thief's possession. Both of these practices produce an unseen factor that the money carries with it; just because we can't see it, doesn't mean it isn't present. The money you have is likewise marked with invisible intention. When you become aware of the unseen power behind your "money thoughts" you can consciously shift the power of producing money back to yourself.

What kind of *intention* is imprinted on the money you carry? Does it come from a wellspring of positive, happy thoughts and actions, or is there something strained or sad about it? It never is about how hard you work for your money, but how you *feel* about the work you do. A person who is working two and three jobs can keep the inflow upbeat and positive, and someone with one, lucrative but miserable job, can have seriously tainted inflow.

I have a friend who works three jobs. He has a regular job as a dispatcher from six AM to three PM. At three-thirty he coaches soccer at his son's school. On Saturdays he teaches specialized exercise classes for physically challenged children. His first job pays his living expenses and he brings his positive personality to work. His second and third jobs, both paid, are more labors of love. He enjoys the spectrum of his life and each segment feeds the other. He puts his earnings from the second and third jobs into designated funds. The diversity of employment brings him great joy and he generously spreads it around. He also volunteers his extra time to church activities. He always has enough energy for all of his pursuits. It is supplied to him in return for his labors.

Acquisition is a two-step process. Money comes wedded to maintenance. Once we acquire something we are obliged to maintain it. If we purchase a bicycle, we have to service it. If we buy a house, we need to preserve it. When the pen we buy runs out of ink, maintenance is called for. Of course, we could just throw used items out and replace them, but when we choose that course of action we may be wasteful and not renewing our resources on the physical and spiritual planes. Not wise: There is a natural law that ultimately exacts payment for waste and rewards conservation.

The amount of money you acquire is determined by a great number of factors, many of them personal choices. Some salaries are paid based on the level of education you've had. Others are paid based on your accomplishments. Some money is handed down from one generation to the next and some is won in a game of chance. To a certain extent you have control over how much you make. You can get an MBA and know that an entry-level position at Such and Such Corporation will pay you X thousands of dollars more per year. You can also work at many types of jobs at a minimum wage and that will bring you in X thousands of dollars per year. The most highly educated individual is free to earn the minimum wage if he or she chooses to. Education doesn't guarantee salary, but it certainly improves the options for acquiring it. If you want to increase your income, you may need to take stock of your qualifications and retool them for today's marketplace.

But it is not the only way. Entrepreneurs and inventors can make money with an idea. Chefs can make money with a

66

secret recipe. Manufacturers can make money with a product. There is no end to the ways we can make money. And, there is no limit to the ways in which we *manage* the money we make.

Terry Cole-Whittaker wrote an article in *The Science of Mind* magazine recounting the story of a Hollywood talent manager who wasn't doing very well in his business. One day he became inspired to change his emphasis. Instead of worrying so much about himself and his own income, he began to think about the welfare of his clients, and what actions or decisions would be good for them. He put his clients' needs ahead of his own desires. His clients were at the forefront of his thinking, his planning and his actions. Very quickly his business began to turn around and he found himself making more money than he had ever imagined. New clients were flocking to him. His business not only increased but he was able to achieve a new level of personal satisfaction and happiness. By the very act of putting others before himself he changed his mind and therefore his results.

That is why it is so important to investigate *acquisition*. The following is a clarification exercise for you to do and use as grist for your mind mill.

> *Part One: Close your eyes and think for a moment about a blank slate. There is a piece of chalk sitting next to the slate. You pick it up and write your description for feeling happy and satisfied at the end of the day. What activities have taken place? How have you spent the hours? Take a few minutes to write on your blackboard. Allow yourself to luxuriate in this mental activity.*

> *Part two: Have you thought about money during this time? If so describe the influx. Did it come as a job, a windfall, a gift, or something else entirely? Did the money affect your happiness one way or the other?*

Again, take a few moments to consider your responses to these questions. You may want to write down your feelings about this exercise. It suggests linkages about happiness and money that might be helpful to you. It is absolutely possible to have your means of acquisition aligned with your feelings of happiness, worth and satisfaction. When this occurs you have achieved a healthy congruency and your Money Model is shaping up nicely.

If you feel that there is a disconnect between how you make your money and your description of happiness, that only means that there is work to be done. It is up to you to figure out how to narrow the gap between the two. (If you stop telling yourself there is no way, you will find the way.)

Can you directly connect your feelings of happiness with the manner in which you acquire money? Do you feel it is important?

> *How easy and yet how mistaken it is to be influenced by the "another day, another dollar" syndrome. Let your work, whatever it may involve, be an outworking of the creative flow, engaged in through shear joy of fulfilling your divine nature. You will prosper, and you should do so, but it will not be because you have "made money in your job." The work in the job is the means by which you build a consciousness of giving, which in turn gives rise to an outworking or receiving flow.*
> – Eric Butterworth.

First we must give and after that we will receive. It may sound a little convoluted at first, but listen to these words from a Harvard professor,

> *The University pays me for doing what I would gladly do for nothing, if I could afford it.*

Does this statement accurately describe your means of employment? What would need to change in order for you to say it? What kind of work would you gladly do for nothing, if you could afford it? We're not talking about sitting on the beach with a pina colada in your hand - although I am sure there is someone who makes a fine living doing just that - we're discussing what you might do as a contributing member of society in the world today if you didn't have to worry about money.

My mother exemplified this statement beautifully. She had worked as a secretary in General Douglas MacArthur's base in Brisbane, Australia, during WWII. My father was stationed in Brisbane and that is how they met. She was accustomed to working full time when she married my father and moved to the US with him after the war. Once I was in school, my mother wanted to return to the work force because she missed the camaraderie of the workplace and she wanted to do something besides housework. She was an outgoing person and liked to be around other people. She answered an ad in the local paper for a part-time clerk in a jewelry store. She was hired on the spot and began working Monday, Wednesday and Friday every week.

There was nothing exceptional about my mother working. The exception was in how she performed on the job. The owner and his wife showed her the ropes and she learned about stones, gems, gold, silver, engraving, ring sizing, pearls and the difference between genuine and synthetic. She was smart, bubbly with the customers, and always deferred to the expertise of the owner if she didn't have the answer. When she wasn't waiting on customers she was polishing silver, straightening displays, restocking the shelves, organizing the wrapping materials, and cataloging new merchandise. She never sat still. The owner's wife would take a break for a smoke, but not my mom. She arrived ready to work, never drank a cup of coffee on the job, took short lunch breaks and occupied her shift by doing something above and beyond her job description. The owner and his wife were in awe. They had never hired anyone as diligent as my mother. They respected her and they openly admitted that they learned from her.

In short order my parents became fast friends with the jewelry store owner and his wife. They came to our house for dinner and we went to theirs. As this flourishing friendship grew, I was allowed to go to the jewelry store after school. Three days a week I walked from my grade school to the jewelry store to wait for my mother to get off work and drive me home. Her enthusiasm and dedication was contagious. I found myself slipping behind the counters to help out when the customers outnumbered the clerks. I followed my mother's lead. I organized, stacked, counted, polished and even wrapped packages during the busy season. I was too young to be paid for my work, but I was greatly appreciated.

Spurred on by my mother's example, I learned how to engrave, repair jewelry, change watchbands, and a host of other bling-related talents. Eventually the owner sold his store, and a competitor down the street snapped up my mother. She went to work for a new jewelry store owning couple and they became even closer friends. They accepted me as part of the package and three days a week they got both of us.

Once again, my mother dazzled them with her extraordinary work ethic. Suddenly no one was sitting down on the job or eating pie behind the counter anymore. They were all following my mother's lead. Business picked up. Customers from the previous store followed my mother to her new location. She brought sincerity and joy to her job. She loved going to work because she adored selling jewelry. Sometimes her salary went right back into the coffers of the owners because of purchases she made. She thrived on her gems.

I benefited from the new job, too. As I got older the owners offered to pay me for my help thereby creating days off for the owner's wife. We had such a good time working that many days she decided to stay and not take the time off after all. She enjoyed the new spirit at work.

My mother was an excellent sales person. Her enthusiasm sold more rings and bracelets than they'd ever sold before. The owner was a watchmaker by trade, but with my mother's bubbly ways, he was soon investing in more jewelry stock. The merchandise was flying out the door.

After 5 years of working together, they offered my mother a partnership. She became part owner of a thriving enterprise all because she gave and gave of herself, well over the top, beyond expectations, and with effervescent joy. It was a thrill to watch her in action. Her conduct was not only inspiring but obviously rewarding: she seriously glittered when she walked.

Acquisition came easily for my mother because her joy was the dominant factor. She thought about other people first, and she made sure their needs were met before her own. I learned so much from her. Her style is engraved in my mind. I remember asking her one day why she never took a break. She looked at me quizzically and said. "I'm on their time not mine." She meant it. If she was being compensated for her time, she was going to make sure her employers got every dime's worth of her day.

Mother never bragged about her level of commitment, she never expected anyone else to follow in her footsteps; she just did what she did because she was grateful for the opportunity and felt a joyous sense of positive obligation to those who paid her money for her time. She was an awesome employee to behold; and a terrific silent teacher!

Her example has served me well. I developed an ingrained respect for compensation of any kind. If I am expected to be at work at a certain time, I'll show up early. Marty Feldman, the British comedian, reinforced that lesson. When I was a stage manager at CBS in Hollywood, I was assigned to the "Cher" show. (Post *Sonny and Cher*). Marty Feldman was to be a guest on the show. When I arrived for work that day (as the junior stage manager my job was to unlock the studio and turn on the lights before anyone else arrived) Marty was waiting outside the studio door. I looked at my watch and apologized for being tardy, though I really wasn't. He smiled and told me that he always showed up early for his call. I asked him why he did that. He replied, "Because I make a lot of money, and it's the very least I can do for those who make less but work harder."

I was deeply touched by his generosity. For the rest of the day I couldn't do enough for him. *Mr. Feldman, may I get you some more coffee? Mr. Feldman, do you need a soda? Mr. Feldman is there anything else we can do to make your time with us more pleasant?"* And I meant every word of it. He was a gentleman. He respected his job he respected his compensation, and he respected the people he worked with. He brought a sense of dignity to the stage, just as my mother did to her job in the jewelry store.

> *There is no job with a future in it; the future is in the one who does the job.*
> – Eric Butterworth.

So how can you foster that? How can you discover within yourself the prosperity consciousness that allows you to say you would do the job anyway, even if they didn't pay you for it? How can you give attention to the ways and the means of the acquisition of your money? I don't have your answers. But perhaps this next exercise can point you in the right direction.

Exercise:

Please take a moment and allow yourself to answer the following questions. Write your answers - it is an important part of the process for change.

> *What do I believe about money?*
> *How important is money to me?*
> *Do I understand the visible and the invisible nature of money?*
> *Do I believe and understand how giving is the first step to receiving?*
> *I understand prosperity is:_____*
> *What can I shift or change in my life to invite in more prosperity:*
> *Do I believe myself worthy of having more abundance?*
> *Am I willing to change my job so it becomes more connected to my purpose and my talents?*
> *How do I honestly respond to the following statement by Ralph Waldo Emerson:*
>
> > *No matter what your work, let it be your*
> > *own. No matter what your occupation, let*
> > *what you are doing be organic. Let it be*
> > *in your bones. In this way you will open*
> > *the door by which the affluence of heaven*
> > *and earth shall stream into you.*
>
> *What do I need to do every day to remember prosperity comes from within?*
> *What do I need to remove from my life that is limiting my consciousness?*
> *What occupation would I choose if I didn't have to be paid for it?*

The secret of achieving prosperity lies in so vividly keeping yourself centered in the inner focus of affluence that you literally exude the consciousness of it.

– Eric Butterworth

Affirmations are powerful tools for staking your claim to the riches that are awaiting you. Read these with genuine emotion and notice how they shift your consciousness toward a greater acceptance of your prosperity.

Sample affirmations:

A) Today I gently affirm my right to the gifts of this world. I align myself with my true purpose and I invite new information into my heart so that I may clearly understand my role on earth. I open my mind and my heart to the unlimited riches of this world as I give first - knowing that I will then also receive. As my consciousness expands, I embody the principle of prosperity and exude confidence, love and joy to everyone I meet and in everything I do.

B) Today I open up to the fullness of the Spirit within me. As this Spirit moves through me it accomplishes all of the work I am appointed to do in a manner of ease and grace. I experience life as a blessing. I engage my inner wisdom as my guide as I consciously communicate with the powers of the Universe. Light shines through me in all of my activities. I am filled with goodness and my supply is unlimited.

Now, please compose your own affirmation (positive statement) for the ways in which you want to acquire your money in the future.

The man who can't dance thinks the band is no good.
– Polish Proverb

Chapter Ten
Lesson 9:
Discipline

To attain emotional security each of us has to develop two critical capabilities: the ability to live with uncertainty, and the ability to delay gratification in favor of long-range goals.
– Denis Whitley

Once we have acquired something of value, whether it is gold, a golden object, or folding money, our next thoughts turn to the best use and preservation of our new possession.

Discipline is concerned with the intentions we have about our acquisitions and the actions we are willing to take in order to preserve what we have acquired. The word discipline includes within it the word *disciple* which simply means "a learner." The original application of the word *discipline* was gentle: "orderly conduct as a result of training." For our purposes, the gentle definition of discipline is a thought-out system for governing our financial behavior which is easily put into action.

The initial interpretation of the word was centered in education and the application of lessons learned. For some today *discipline* may be a word burdened with negative connotations, but that's exactly where the power of the mind comes in. Like everything else we have previously discussed, discipline occurs in the mind as well as in the physical world. If you have experienced *discipline* as physical abuse, or a limitation of your freedom, or behavior, then there is some work for you to do to reverse that mindset, and thereby change your results. Discipline ought to be a positive and beautiful quality. It is the high octane fuel for the wealth machine; discipline *plus* focus equals prosperity.

If you suddenly win the lottery – especially if you win the lottery - you will want to use the tool of discipline to handle what you acquire, or you will watch your fortune disappear as quickly as it arrived. We are reminded of the Lotto winners featured in People magazine, who are back in exactly the same place they were before they won their windfall. Their winnings slipped right through their fingers.

The components of discipline are preparation, coaching, priming, guiding, method, and approach. Discipline does not refer to the crabby old school marm wielding her ruler and beating the living bejezesus out of your knuckles when you missed a word on your spelling test. Nor is it some crusty sergeant yelling in your face at boot camp. Rather, it is a way of thinking that allows you to establish your priorities and habitually follow them to achieve your goals. When you look at it that way, doesn't discipline take on a whole new meaning?

I'll never forget a time when my parents and I were vacationing in California with family friends. We were driving up Pacific Coast Highway and the signs intrigued us: "Condos for sale, gorgeous ocean views." We took the right turn into the flag-lined driveway and headed up the hill to tour the model home. The location was wonderful. The condos were still under construction, but, "if they bought today", Dad and Mother would be able to pick the location, the view and even the carpet colors. It was a magnificent property in Laguna Niguel. My dad was very excited. He and my mom had a quiet discussion and my dad signed up to buy one on the spot. We left after a couple of hours and my dad was beaming about his purchase.

When we returned to our beach hotel that night, Dad began to do the math. He read and re-read the papers he received at signing, and after a restless night's sleep, decided that the monthly payments would squeeze him just a little too tightly for his own comfort. He was broken-hearted when he announced his findings at breakfast. I watched my mother's face as she listened to the suggestion that they rescind the deal and not purchase the property. I could see the disappointment for both of them, but they decided together that the extra payment would hinder their lives too much. They were concerned about the cost of my schooling and the upcoming expenses for the business they wanted to expand.

I remember that my father was genuinely embarrassed when he called the sales agent and said he wanted to cancel the purchase. The sales agent gave him some grief in an attempt to shame him back into the deal, but my father held steadfast. He was aware that under California law you had a 3-day buyer's remorse clause, and he exercised it. He lost his $1,000 deposit, but he gained a sense of balance and harmony for his life so that he could do what he truly wanted to do - without undue pressure.

Yes, that property tripled in value within the first five years and today it is worth over a million dollars. However, my father decided not to pay the emotional price of making steep monthly payments. He was smart. He knew his budgetary limits. Ultimately, the investment in my education and his business brought in much more.

My father knew it would be important for me to learn the value of an earned dollar. We lived in the Northwest and during the summer the adjacent farms supplied the local markets with fruit and berries. He encouraged me to amass my fortune by working in the fields. And so, I became one of the many local kids who picked strawberries during June. A rusty, old, retired school bus picked us up on the main road by our house at 6 AM. We traveled an hour, gathering other berry-pickers on our way. We arrived in the fields by 7:30 and picked berries until about 4. We were allowed a half-hour lunch break and we were required to bring our own lunch because there were no meal wagons on wheels back then. The rickety bus delivered us home about 6 PM. We made $2.50 for each flat of berries and as we handed our full flat to the foreman, we got our ticket punched. At the end of the week we turned in our tickets and they paid us in cash. By Friday afternoon we were sun-burnt and exhausted. Our hands were bright red from picking thousands of berries and our equally reddened skin proved we'd spent some serious time outdoors. But we also had our money.

Strawberry picking lasted through June and maybe into the first week of July. The raspberry crop followed on the heels of the strawberries and we continued for another few weeks during the prime season. Raspberries were more difficult because the vines were higher and taller. The berries were smaller, so it took more raspberries to fill a flat; yet the pay was the same.

My father offered me a deal. Whatever money I made picking berries was to go into a savings account. At the end of the season, he would match my earnings dollar for dollar. As a reward and an incentive he agreed to buy me the item (transistor radio, typewriter, outfit) I'd had my heart set on.

It was a good deal for a twelve year old. I not only made money, but it was doubled, and I got to have a treat too. No matter how hot that sun was or how much my pre-teen back was aching, I carried on - motivated by the pot of gold my father placed at the end of my berry-colored rainbow. Most of the other kids spent their weekly earnings on treats and entertainment, but my wages went into the bank.

I picked berries for three years and I watched as my savings and the interest on it grow and grow. Every time I received money as a gift, or earned a little extra cash, I added it to that savings account. Fifteen years later the money in that same account became the down payment for my dream house. To this day strawberries hold a very special place in my heart.

Watching my father operate in the world, and seeing the results of his Principles first hand, I started to take a few notes. At first the notes were scattered hither and yon, but eventually I organized and began to faithfully practice them. His wisdom and discipline has paid off for me. Let me now share with you what he taught me.

These are the nine time-tested **Money Maxims** that you can apply to your life to produce prosperity:

> #1. Save more money than you spend. (No excuses. Make it happen!)
> #2. Never deplete your principal; not even for special occasions.
> #3. Live beneath your means. (No matter how uncomfortable it may temporarily be.)
> #4. Never lend money; just be willing to *give away* what you can afford to lose.
> #5. The Road to Ruin is paved with plastic credit cards.
> #6. Put on your own oxygen mask before you attempt to assist others.
> #7. Today's choice becomes tomorrow's reality. Substitute immediate gratification for long-term fulfillment.
> #8. Live fully in the moment but act wisely for the future.
> #9. Give back: 10% of your money and 10% of your time to the sources of your spiritual inspiration.

Along with the money lessons I was constantly learning from my father and my mother, these Money Maxims have formed the basis of thinking and practice that have allowed me to be in the driver's seat of my finances all of my life.

Maxim #1: Save more money than you spend.

I can hear the squeals of protest as you read this. No matter who you are, what you are doing or how old you are, you must apply this rule to your financial life. Take the time to look at where and how you spend your money. It may not be easy, or comfortable, but it doesn't have to be hideous either. Circumstances are only temporary and you can change them anytime you want.

In an article for the Kansas City Star entitled "He knows firsthand: Spenders can become Savers,"[1] Jillian Mincer wrote:

> *David Bach calls it the "latte factor." He described a 22 year-old woman who insisted she couldn't afford to save. But she discovered she was spending about $10 a day on coffee and snacks. If she cuts down enough to save $2,000 a year and invests the money at 11 percent, she would have $2 million by the time she retired.*

If you are skeptical, Google "latté factor" and then go to the "latté factor calculator" and see how much you spend and how much you could earn by simply saving $20 a week. No matter how long you have snoozed, the numbers are enough to wake you up without the caffeine. If you saved $20 per week and put it into an account that brought you 10% annual interest, you would have $506,325.88 in 40 years. Don't let the concept of 40 years frighten you. It's never too early or too late to begin. Imagine for a moment that you saved $100 a week for 40 years: your accumulated savings would be $1,110,769.76. Pretty impressive and not impossible. It all boils down to what you do with what you have.

Do you remember what you had for breakfast or lunch two days ago? Most of us do not. So, if you do NOT purchase the "latté" you're probably not going to even remember it in a day

[1]"He Knows Firsthand: Spenders Can Become Savers," Jillian, Mincer, The Kansas City Star, May 2, 1999

or two. You need to begin thinking forward. "Will I *remember* this in two days? In two days will my *need* still be there?" "Will *this* still be *useful* in two days?" If the answer is "no" then *don't spend your money on it*! This is the simple way to curb your spending and begin accumulating wealth. The pesky child inside of you *wants* to satisfy its whim in the moment. All kids do. You'll always have "wants" circling around you like insatiable gnats. If we say "yes" to the gnats on a regular basis we'll have the bank balance of a gnat.

What *will* set you apart from the crowd, and what is one of the *key reasons* why I can say that I am financially independent today, is the positive choice to say "no" to forgettable expenditures. Flavored coffees, bagels, candy bars, bags of cookies, donuts, blah, blah, blah, are all *forgettable expenses*. You won't remember them in two days, you probably won't remember them in two hours, so why not put that money to a better use for yourself and your future?

I can hear you thinking, "But what if I want to enjoy a designer coffee? I work hard. I deserve a treat." You're right. You do. The secret is to control it. Have your latte only once a week. The rest of the week, drink free coffee and put what you would have spent on designer coffees in the bank. It's going to net you a much more memorable payoff in the long run.

What else? Lunches and dinners. You'll save *so much money* if you don't eat out. Make your own lunch. Ignore what other people may say or think. Ask yourself, "Will this person be in my life when I have the prosperity to live my life at the level I want to? Or, will they be long gone?" Don't let their comments today affect tomorrow's prosperity. If you take your own lunch to school, work, whatever, you'll have extra time to walk, read, meditate, or listen to music. You'll be fully able to enjoy some soul restoring time and return to work refreshed. You'll also avoid those forgettable office conversations which too often are nothing more than an exchange of idle gossip.

Okay, now that you're skipping your forgettable expenditures, and bringing your lunch, what's next? Each week, *consciously put that money away.* Create the habit of regularly depositing that money into your savings account (or better yet, money market account, where you will receive higher interest). You'll see that by setting aside your fleeting momentary desires, and putting the money to work for you, you can accumulate a surprising amount in a short amount of time.

The next step in putting aside more than you spend is to create a budget for yourself. In your work with this book you've become accustomed to value-based thinking. You put more value on what you can *save* than on what you can *spend* in the moment. You will most likely need to review and adjust your living expenses. Your overhead should not require more than 25% of your paycheck. Be willing to buy less and compromise on quantity - substituting *quality* instead. Place a value on your incidental purchases by considering how long you will remember them. Make a commitment to yourself to curb your impulses and follow your budget.

One of the easiest ways to stay on track with your budget is to operate on a cash-only basis. Cut up the credit cards and stop writing checks or using your debit card. Withdraw *exactly* your budgeted amount of cash each week and use that cash to get you through. If you over-spend once and find yourself short at the end of the week, it will be crystal clear what you need to avoid in the future. When you have to pull out cash instead of swiping a piece of plastic, it makes you really think about what you are spending your precious money on.

Our subconscious mind actually enjoys the guidelines that our conscious mind sets. Given direction, the subconscious mind performs in accordance with what is set out for it. There is no guess work, just straightforward progress. In setting up new behavioral and financial guidelines, you are doing yourself a gigantic favor. There is no guess work. You become the Pied Piper of your own prosperity. When you set forth the directives all your parts follow suit. The result is harmony, agreement and prosperity. Highlight this paragraph and read it over and over until its yours.

Maxim #2. *Never deplete principal; not even for special occasions.*

Do not raid your piggy bank, your savings account, or your stock portfolio, to pay for a triple-action vacuum or a vacation in the Bahamas. What you put aside stays aside; that's the rule. Create separate untouchable accounts for the things you want to do or accomplish. If you want to take scuba lessons, put the money aside, and save until you have enough for your lessons and your gear. If you want a vacation in Barbados, save up in a separate account until you have enough for the trip. So many people in this country are stressed-out over the supposed-to-be-unstressful vacations they have charged on their credit cards. "But I deserve this vacation...." Sure you do. We all do. But you also deserve the serenity of paying for it in advance, so you can truly enjoy the experience.

This may take all the apparent fun out of spring break, but spring break will come and go, your future lies ahead. What you can do while you're waiting for the account to become large enough for the vacation is be creative. Find local activities and local getaways. Discipline your desires and impulses into having a great time for less money and wait until you're fully prepared financially to take that vacation.

A dear friend of mine was a bartender for most of his adult life. He made a practice of living on his salary and putting all of his tips into savings. He had plenty of fun, and with his Mel Gibson looks and dashing blue eyes, he was the heartthrob of the bar. He made his workplace a fun place to be. He adored people, made them feel welcome, remembered their names and what they liked to drink, and, above all, he was discreet. His tip jar runneth over. But he didn't rush out to spend it. He saved. One fine day he took a look at his account balance and put some money down on a house. His salary covered the rent and taxes, so he continued to save his tips and bought a second house. During the day he remodeled the houses and at night he worked in the bar. When he rented out the second house he suddenly had two streams of income. He saved more and bought some land with an even more spectacular view.

When he finally decided to retire from the bar routine his future was set. He had multiple streams of income, a house that was paid for, and investment property to rent or sell as he chose. He was smart. He never lacked for entertainment, fun or excitement. He traveled, he played sports, he dated and he prospered. Everyone can do it. Everyone, no matter what the economic conditions appear to be, can do the same thing my friend did. Planning and sticking to the formula, no matter what, is the key.

You must follow your own rules. You must save for your ultimate freedom like my friend did. You must keep yourself from withdrawing "a little here and there" from your master account. If you want to do something, study something, travel somewhere, or have a shopping spree, save up for it and when you have the cash go for it. Do not drain your long-term assets for short-term satisfaction.

Hands off! Resist the temptation to dilute your principal. Let it expand and grow until you are ready to reinvest it in something greater. My friend did that. He was brilliant. He now lives like a king, travels with his gorgeous wife, and possesses the inner peace and happiness we all crave. Nobody handed it to him. He made the best of his job, and created a spectacular life. He's awesome. You can be too.

Maxim #3. Live beneath your means.

First you save, then you leave the principal alone to grow. You accomplish this by always living beneath your means. It isn't as hideous as it may seem.

Remember our four friends? Two spent every nickel they earned and two saved for the future. The two who practiced living beneath their means have freedom and choice today. The two who spent like there was no tomorrow didn't create an emancipated today. You don't have to have all the bells, whistles, laptops and fancy cars that the magazines claim you need to have in order to live a full life. No one was ever made permanently happy or felt spiritually fulfilled in the long term by driving a snazzy sports car. Use your money as energy for creating the future you desire for yourself and your children.

Unleash your creative genius. Look for new ways to enjoy yourself. Do not succumb to the temporary allure of advertising campaigns, commercials, and sexy billboards. Take charge of your inner self and enlarge the scope of your life by exploring carefully and choosing wisely. You can live beneath your means even if you make ten dollars an hour. You *should* also live beneath your means if you make one hundred dollars an hour! The maxim applies to everyone regardless of age or status.

While you are in your teens, twenties and thirties, your mission is to build. It is a time to lay the foundations for your life so that when you are older, you can relax and enjoy. If you fritter your income away on every whim and temporary desire, you will have nothing to show for your years of work but an enormous volume on the history of frittering.

If you're past your twenties, thirties, forties or fifties, you can still apply these principles and maxims to your life. According to the experts, the latest science suggests that we may live to be 100 or older. Unless you are already there, you should prepare for the future. You may feel as though you've worked hard all of your life and have earned the right to luxury. We all do, but if you do not have a cushion you should start building one today. Remember the world continues to change, and costs are rising; no matter what your age, you need to hedge for your future. Predictably you will live to a ripe old age. Plan so that when the time comes you'll have a cushion. The maxims for prosperity apply to all ages.

Maxim #4. *Never lend money; just be willing to give away what you can afford to lose.*

Banks were created to lend and collect money, you weren't. Never lend money. I can hear your mind ticking away, "But what if they *really need it?*" "I'm not a person who can say no." "After all *it's my sister!*" I understand exactly how you feel, so let's explore this maxim a little further.

Money has two types of energy: physical and intangible. When you have money many people in your life believe you should share it with them. They often believe *"What's mine is mine and what's yours is mine, too."* There are those who think they are entitled to your money just because you have some and they don't. Please hear this: You are under no obligation, spiritual or material, to give away what you have acquired. No matter what *anyone* tells you. This is not selfish, it's smart.

The rule is this: Never *lend* money; just be willing to *give away* what you are prepared to kiss good-bye. Family members and strangers alike are individually and collectively governed by this rule. If you want to help a friend or a family member, do so, but don't expect to see the money again. If you follow this rule two things will happen for you: Because you gave it freely, the gift has no power to ruin a relationship. You also won't have to live in fear about getting the money back - so your gift can be freely and generously given. Banks are in the business of lending and collecting money. They lend it for business, for emergencies, and for improvements. They ask that the borrower follow certain criteria for accepting their money. They are quite happy to loan money to you, providing you pay them back and they can profit from their good faith and trust in you. If a person is coming to you, instead of the bank, for money could it be that they:

> Are just lazy and don't want to go through the paperwork of a bank loan;
> Can't *qualify* for a loan;
> Have a history of bad debts;
> Have never, ever been able to manage money;
> Think you're a softie.

Why then would you ever want to lend them money? Why would you want to contribute to the reinforcement of their bad habits? Why would you want to become their banker? Why would you put yourself through that?

Feeling guilty about this? Having trouble swallowing the concept? Think of it this way: You fall into the category of enabler if you hand them free money and allow them to temporarily plug up the hole in their leaky boat, without repairing their underlying problem. It's no different than serving a recovering alcoholic a drink. Lending people money does *not* generally help them; it usually just furthers their unhealthy financial patterns. If they moan and groan and attempt to make you feel stingy, or tight-fisted, so what? Stand your ground. Be pleasant and supportive of their requests and then point them in the direction of legitimate financial institutions. You didn't get them into this situation; you needn't feel responsible for bailing them out.

Maxim #5. The Road to Ruin is paved with plastic credit cards.

Another cardinal rule of prosperity consciousness is to pay cash for everything you purchase. Don't buy anything unless you have the cash for it. You have to agree that you will have *NO MORE CREDIT CARDS*. Here's some mind-staggering information from Credit Card Consumers of America:

- *Total US consumer debt (which includes installment debt, but not mortgage debt) reached $2.46 Trillion in June 2007, up from $2.398 Trillion at the end of 2006 (Source: Federal Reserve)*
- *Total US consumer revolving debt reached $904 Billion in June 2007, up from $879 billion at the end of 2006 (Source: Federal Reserve)*
- *The median U.S. household income is currently $43,200 and the typical family's credit card balance is now almost 5 percent of their annual income. (Source: Federal Reserve)*
- *8.3 percent of households owe $9,000 or more on their cards (Source: MSN Money)*
- *Approximately 40 percent of credit card users paid their balance in full each month in 2006 (Source: Federal Reserve Bank of Philadelphia)*

Have you been contributing to the statistics? One of the truest things about credit card debt is that, by the time the bill arrives, you've forgotten most of the items you charged. Food, movies, and lattes are ancient history when it comes time to pay. Limit your expenses. Pay cash for what you buy. It's cheaper in the long run and you have the luxury of control.

If you still insist upon using a credit card, there are two rules to follow: *Pay them forward.* In other words, *DEPOSIT* a certain amount into your credit card account and only spend what you've put in. No cheating! If you DO use a credit card, then you absolutely have to *pay it off in full* when you receive the bill each month. I use a credit card for the airline miles it provides, and I pay it off every month. I pay ahead of the due date so I won't incur finance charges. Late fees can run up ($25-50.00) and the interest on the charges can hit double digits. Why on earth would you want to give your extra money to the bank just because you didn't pay your bill on time? If you deposited $40 a month (a typical late fee) and let it build you would have $84,681.52 in 30 years. Why would you give that money away? Your banker isn't going to write you a thank you note or put a plaque on the wall with your name on it. Start keeping a calendar. Make a note about when to pay your bills so you avoid finance charges. Or, you can hang a picture of a smiling banker above your desk and just know that you are making him a very happy man, and helping to finance the new addition to the bank, with your late fees.

What's wrong with debit cards? Unless you are willing to faithfully record each purchase as if it were a check, and deduct that amount from your account, cut them up. Have a party, organize a hoe-down, do anything you have to do, but cut them up! Debit cards can fool you into thinking you can spend when you really shouldn't. Only use that debit card to draw money out of the bank - as budgeted – and you'll be a lot happier and richer.

Maxim #6. Put on your own oxygen mask before you attempt to assist others.[2]

The undeniable reality of this statement is that you have to be responsible for yourself first, before you do for others. You need insure that you have the oxygen of money, and are breathing well, before you presume to save another. This does not mean you become a narcissist, it means that you assume responsibility for your fiscal life and let others do the same for theirs.

Using sound management for your finances, you will be able to function independently and strongly in life. If you are waiting for others to increase or manage your finances you are invalidating your personal resource power. Once you obtain a stream of income, no matter if you are ten years old, begin to put the Money Model and the Maxims into play. The best gift you can give a person is to teach them to manage their own money, otherwise you are encouraging them to be careless with it and to become a money fritterer.

When you get married try this approach: bring your own money into the relationship, but keep it separate and manage it yourself. Create one joint account into which both of you contribute, but don't merge all of your resources in a checkbook that *you* don't solely govern. For some of you this statement will appear to argue against the basic concept of marriage, co-mingling, and creating a life *together*. But money is one of the key reasons marriages break up. If a couple does not take the time to talk about money *before* marriage and agree on spending patterns (and most of us don't because we are too busy falling in love), it is easy for one or the other to trip the balance – especially if all the resources are in one account.

[2] Inspired by Pam Young & Peggy Jones, *The Sidetracked Home Executives*

When each party manages his or her own resources and *contributes* to the funds that support life together, the relationship - and the money – has breathing room. National statistics report that fifty percent of marriages end in divorce. Dividing resources and possessions is a costly legal process. Money kept separate insures an easier resource settlement. Of course there are many factors to consider; whether one spouse remains home to care for the children; whether one spouse makes a lot more money than the other; whether one spouse is trained to manage assets.

All these factors and many more like them, require careful consideration. But, the concept of separate accounts remains the same. No matter what happens, *manage your own money.* I have a dear friend who went into two separate marriages with the intention of proving her love by co-mingling funds. What she got to prove *twice* was that love may not last, but the bills do. Both times she was stuck paying off those joint accounts.

The object of this maxim is to be responsible for yourself. Put on your own oxygen mask first, before helping or co-mingling with others. If this goes against your grain, read the Maxim again and then create your own scenario; one in which you benefit from this plan. Put the romance and the storybook ideal away for just a moment and look at the reality of a balance sheet. There is nothing redeeming or heroic about paying off someone else's Visa bills.

Maxim #7. *Today's choice becomes tomorrow's reality. Substitute immediate gratification for long-term fulfillment.*

It is simply astonishing how quickly money grows when you leave it alone. If you continue adding to the basic fund the exponential growth is thrilling. Your life is busy and full of distractions so it's pretty painless to save money and let it accumulate. Time passes quickly and you'll hardly be aware of what you don't have. You will be pleased to see what your certificate of deposit has earned in the bank while you were out living life. You need to get in the habit of getting *more excited* over interest than you are over the newest fashion craze or the latest box office blockbuster.

Placing "tomorrow" in your vision sphere allows you to take an extra moment to make a decision about the activity or thing you are about to engage in. Ask yourself,

> *Do I need it, or do I just want it in the moment?*
> *Will it contribute to my goals and my overall financial plan?*
> *What lasting effect will remain tomorrow, next week, next month?*
> *What else might I do instead?*
> *What would happen if I saved the money instead of spending it?*
> *What would I actually gain if I put this money to work for me?*

Get creative. There are so many things to do in this world that don't cost money. Break the habit of going to all the first-run movies. That mega-hit movie will be on DVD in no time. Eat at home before going to your special movie so you aren't tempted to buy $15.00 worth of popcorn and soda at the show. Take walks, meet in the park, have picnics. Spend time in nature. Take your food along with you. Teach all of these ideas to your children.

Shop only when it falls into your plan. If you are depressed, bored or antsy, *do not* go shopping. Go to the beach, or the mountains, or the park or somewhere to fill your soul that does not deplete your finances. These sprees may occupy some time for you, but they will not contribute to your financial strength. Take your shopping jones and put it to use by volunteering your time at a local charity. Malls are filled with lonely, depressed, bored people; do not become one of them. Make better use of your time and energy.

Maxim #8. *Live fully in the moment but act wisely for the future.*

After my dad received his electrical engineering degree he was hired by G.E. to work for them and increase his field knowledge at the same time. Being young, newly married, honorably released from military service, and about to be a father, he jumped at the opportunity and moved back to New York with his Aussie bride.

He learned a great deal about management from the G.E. training and he learned more about his trade, ingenious avenues for putting his knowledge to work, and clever applications of the various products G.E. made. He learned about everything from light bulbs and appliances to giant oil refining machines and their eight thousand respective parts.

At the end of the training he was teeming with knowledge, so he packed up once again and moved back west; where he took a job as an electrical designer with a family-owned company in a small Pacific-northwest city.

My father was a personable guy, easy to get along with, and good at his job. When he met with potential clients, he offered to design the lighting for their store, house, mall, library, campus, or market at no charge. The practice was unheard of in his day. It proved to be an excellent way to entice new customers. The profit from the electrical labor and parts would more than cover his design time and the fulfillment would come directly from the sales force. Of course, because of the free design, most of the bids were happily accepted. My father's expertise and personality quickly expanded the company.

Soon my dad was not only designing the electrical layouts and blue prints for new construction, he was also made manager of the sales team. Why not keep it all under one hat? Design plus fulfillment was the name of his game.

The company prospered and, as it did, my father couldn't help but notice the family that owned it was far from close knit. Four siblings had inherited the business, but two of the owner-brothers were in constant conflict with each other. My father took note of the rivalry and when one of the brothers decided he wanted out of the business, my father offered to buy his stock. With great diplomacy my father convinced the family it was in their best interest to have him as a partner. They sold him the stock.

A few years later, the company was doing so well that my dad brought on another electrical engineer and increased the sales force. He made sales calls to potential new clients to demonstrate to them how his complimentary design services could save them money and contribute to their businesses.

Soon, because of his G.E. education and his creative tenacity, he attracted the oil refinery machine and parts business, as well as some of the food-packing and fish plants in town. The family members continued to squabble as my father acquired more clients and more stock.

One day Dad was particularly nervous, which wasn't his usual style at all. The family had called a special meeting. They felt my father was running the business *his* way and not listening to the family's direction. They weren't wrong.

The family sat on one side of the conference table; my father sat on the other. They told him they wanted to be apprised more of what was going on. They'd heard in the wind that my dad was planning to add more staff, and to let the women wear slacks to work instead of skirts (of all things!). To top it all they heard he was considering allowing some of the female secretaries, who knew the clients better than some of the new sales*men*, to join the sales force. They demanded that he consult them before allowing such an outrageous thing. They even said they might fire him if he didn't do it their way.

Very calmly, my father said that, as they wished, he would keep them informed. He promised to hold meetings once a week at 7 am and they were all invited to attend. Throats cleared and shuffles were heard in the room: collectively the family was not at all pleased with the invitation or the hour.

Just as the meeting was breaking up, my dad announced he had one more piece of information. They turned eagerly to listen. That was when he quietly informed them that he was the 51% stockholder now and that *his* was the new *family* in charge. They were flabbergasted. Some of them twitched, some jumped up and down in place; others gasped, *"This can't be true! It can't be."* But it was. While they had been squabbling, golfing, vacationing and wagging their fingers at him, my father had been buying-up as much stock as he could from the disgruntled siblings. He'd also been able to purchase the building that the business was renting. None of this was done on the sly; the family was just accustomed to not paying attention, so they never did. They were not good managers. They were used to someone else doing everything for them and as a result, they collectively lost the business. (Refer to Chapter 2 and the Lenape tribe.)

There's more! Within a week the family came to my dad with a proposition. Since the company was no longer owned by *their* family, they asked my father if he wanted to buy the remaining shares. He did. It took a few months to negotiate a fair price; but ultimately everything fell into place. My father secured a bank note to complete the purchase by leveraging the shares he had already purchased in the company. With bank financing he bought the company lock, stock and light bulbs. It was a day to remember for all concerned.

One little man who worked *for* the company accomplished this on a fixed salary. He didn't receive a windfall. He didn't have a big check from his father to help him, he just lived beneath his means, saved every penny he could, built his own house on nights and weekends, and ended up owning the company he worked for in less than fifteen years. He was no more extraordinary than you. But he *was* disciplined.

Acting wisely for the future, combined with living fully in the moment is a highly developed skill - and a keystone to developing wealth. When you live your life fully in the moment you are present for all of the unexpected challenges, joys and opportunities. Taking action with your eye to the future ensures stability in the long term; which allows you to live both spontaneously and securely. What a concept! Keep your life fresh and alive. Find something new to do everyday and do it with great abandon. Wear bright red underpants under your gray three-piece suit. Throw caution to the wind, but *don't* throw your money away.

Maxim #9. *Give back 10% of your money and 10% of your time to the sources of your spiritual inspiration.*

It is essential that you keep your flow flowing. From what source do you receive your inspiration? Who are your teachers? Who or what do you seek out when you need renewal? Contribution oils the gears of your prosperity machine. When you use a resource, you need to replace it. Give 10% of your earnings to the people and places that elevate your spirit and inspire your soul. It could be your church, it could be a website, it could be a school; only you know the sources of your greatest inspiration. Keep that source active and functioning with your contribution so that others may be inspired as you have been. The flow must go on.

Being in show business attracts the wanna-be writer in dentists, waiters, and many others. Throughout my career I was asked by hundreds of people, from all walks of life, to read their TV idea or screenplay. At first, I did because I didn't want to hurt their feelings. I spent hours and hours of my free time reading works that would never be produced, because I wanted to "be nice," and make them happy. Many times the opposite occurred. Not only was I expected to read their work and like it, but there was the expectation that I should get it produced for them as well. If I didn't like it or if I told them that I had no connections in the appropriate genre for them, they got mad. After quite a few years of this vicious cycle, I applied my 10% formula. I give back 10% to my industry, as a tithe. That means that I mentor and help people 10% of the time. Suddenly, the path was clearer and when I reached my 10% I was able to graciously turn down the requests to read the work of hopefuls who, more than likely, I couldn't help.

My 10% rule turned out to be a magnificent creative force in my life. I joined committees within my Guild to assist others on the way up, and mentoring became something I truly enjoyed. I formalized my contribution and was able to stop the drain on my leisure time. Instead of reading someone's unsolicited material, I created a document that explained how show business actually works and the path a newbie needed to follow to get his or her work read by the *right* people, the people who might be able to do something with their material. I listed resources, publications, suggested five books to read, and gave them valuable career advice. This creative solution was a success. Less of my own time was used and the would-be writers were helped and happy with the advice.

The key to this Maxim is giving back. You must do that if you expect effective return. If you try to keep every minute or every penny for yourself, your prosperity will dwindle and eventually stagnate. Stimulate the flow and give back to perpetuate your source. You'll discover the right balance for your own style of tithing.

At the risk of repeating myself: if you are not 22 and you do not have savings, have never followed financial discipline and you're scared to death about how you're going to live; if your deepest fear is ending up homeless, and living on the streets with all of your possessions in a shopping cart, what I'd like you to do, if you find yourself in a tight situation like that, is take a long deep breath - and keep reading.

It is never too late to begin. Your choices must be rigorous and *very* disciplined because you need to make up for some lost time. Nothing is impossible if you are willing to begin. You'll have to apply what you've read beginning now. Read the rest of the chapter and then sit down, get out some paper and go to work. Realistically, list your assets and all your income on one side of the page. On the other, list your expenses. Next, apply the categories and the rules for percentages that you will find in Chapter Eleven on Management. Where are you off the mark? (Keep breathing!)

Sit down with your list as if you were the financial counselor and your list was the client. What would you advise this person to do in order to conform to the rules and Maxims? Remember, it is not you, it is your client. What would you advise them to cut, change, shift or combine in order to create a budget that allowed for savings and growth? This isn't time to fall prey to the "I can'ts" or the "That's impossible's," or the "I don't want to's" this is a time for realism and courage. It's *never* too late! You'll just have to get to work now.

We have covered half the Money Model, the Truths About Money, the Money Maxims and the Principles that govern them. You'll have everything you need to build your wealth base once you read the last four facets of the Money Model.

Remember you could live to be 100. Your future depends on you.

Cheerfulness in most cheerful people is the rich and satisfying result of strenuous discipline.
- Edwin Percy Whipple

Chapter Eleven
Lesson 10:
Exchange

We are here to add what we can to life,
not to get what we can from it.
– William Osler

With Discipline you focus the distribution of your acquired resources. **Exchange** is about how you give and take from the eternal and Universal pool of abundance. It is both a verb and a noun so it refers to the act of swapping one thing for another; to the physical coin of the realm; and to the invisible, underlying truth behind the concept of interchange. As such, the *quality* of the exchange becomes as important as the deed of exchange itself.

To every action there is always opposed an equal
reaction.   – Isaac Newton

It seems simple enough to understand, but it can be tricky.

The path to reciprocity is indirect: reciprocity
ensues from the social capital built by making
contributions to others.   – Wayne Baker

Activating the Law of Reciprocation or Exchange begins in the mind. It's more than giving and getting; it is a spiritual positioning of your mind so as to *extend* yourself and your talents into the world first before looking towards gain.

You cannot give every man or (woman) more in
cash market value than you take from him (her),
but you can give more in use value than the cash
value of the thing you take from him (her).
– Wallace D. Wattles

Here's an example of how it works: The tenant in one of my rental houses sent me an email asking to extend her lease for an additional year. I happily agreed, but shortly thereafter she was diagnosed with a condition that required surgery. She wrote the most thoughtful email telling me of her plight. She said she would honor our agreement if I asked her to, but she really needed to be in another city for the surgery and recuperation period and this would mean terminating her lease seven months earlier than our agreement called for.

I immediately wrote her back and told her I would do anything she needed to do; that her healing came first and we'd adjust accordingly. There were other ways to react. There were other choices I could have made. I could have gotten angry at the termination of the agreement and insisted she abide by the contract she signed. I could have found ways to make her life even more difficult.

I believed there was grace in extending her a gesture of relief. I believed further that there was another person out there just waiting for the opportunity to live in this lovely house. I was not worried. I released this situation freely believing that mutual attraction is a law and it would be fulfilled.

Within hours the doorbell rang and I received a breathtakingly beautiful arrangement of white orchids. The note said, "Thank you for your understanding and consideration." How many of us, diagnosed with a serious illness, would be sending flowers to our landlord? My tenant deserves the credit for this extraordinary gesture. She inspired me to help her even further if I could.

My tenant graciously agreed to show the rental home for me and answer any questions that the potential renters had. Together we found the perfect tenant to take her place. Nary a beat was skipped and all parties were mutually pleased with the outcome.

Take a moment to consider a situation in your life that began with your concern for another and ended up surprising you with a beneficial outcome you couldn't have predicted?

Generosity is a cornerstone of achieving prosperity. We must continually extend our resources and ourselves, and we must do it wisely.

Look back to the Principle we discussed in Chapter Nine. It may have been a little bit harsh to hear the rule: "Don't lend money; give only what you can afford to lose."

We discussed the difficulty of adhering to this maxim in the real world of needy friends and family. But clearly you can see the truth of it. *Give* the money at a level you are able to without damaging yourself, but don't *expect* reciprocation in kind. Your gift then is pure, clean, authentic and not tainted by the worry of whether you'll get it back. Don't lend money unless you are a banker.

When you lend money, instead of giving it freely, you throw yourself under the wheels of the Law of Reciprocation and you inherit the consciousness of *lender* or *expector*. Give generously, and you put yourself in a position to receive more good. All of these actions originate from a joyous spirit - unclouded by the worry of expected return.

> *Take a moment to close your eyes and recall an instance when you gave something out of pure joy, pure love with no attachment to, or expectations for, the outcome.*
>
> *What did you give?*
>
> *To whom did you give it?*
>
> *Recall your feelings in the memory. Did you experience the feeling of pure generosity?*

The ideal goal is to give from this inner sanctum all the time.

> *There is only abundance for the person who focuses on helping and enriching the lives of others with their talents and products in the spirit of love. Find a need and fill it is the secret of wealth.* – Terry Cole-Whittaker

It also serves you to extend the same gift-giving and non-lending consciousness to yourself. Give generously *and* act wisely.

The next chapter on Management will shed more light on the ways and means by which you may accomplish this.

Grant that I may become beautiful in my soul within, and that all my external possessions may be in harmony with my inner self. May I consider the wise to be rich, and may I have such riches as only a person of self-restraint can bear or endure.
– Plato

Chapter Twelve
Lesson 11:
Management

Knowledge is of no value unless you put it into practice
– Heber J. Grant

With the spirit of Exchange deeply imbedded, you move forward into Management. **Management** describes the system by which you apportion your money and the thinking behind it. Management is premeditated allocation for the distribution of your wealth. When you acquire something it requires decision-making. This is the principle behind Management.

It serves you to consider money on two levels: the visible and the invisible. Money is easy to handle when you can see it and feel it. The soul of money is a little more difficult to grasp. When you are paid for your work, you are, in effect, acknowledged with substance (money) for your contribution to the workplace. When you *invest* your money you are rewarded for your faith in the growth of another enterprise. As your faith increases; so does your prosperity simply because you believed in the collective energy of growth and expansion. When you add direction to your faith, you generate more attraction which is all headed back towards you. The power of money lies in its purity as an energetic means of exchange between people and in *your* faith to turn it over to a Universe which can do nothing with it except create more.

Let's explore this idea more deeply. If you purchase a car, along with your acquisition comes required maintenance. Automobile maintenance is best accomplished by regular visits to a professional mechanic, or by spending Sundays in your own garage with a can of Penzoil. (Assuming you know what you're doing under the hood.)

We have acquired enormous desires in this country. Our appetites are enticed by hot commercials and tantalizing ads; our entertainment is bejeweled with consumerism. We are encouraged to buy, buy, buy! What isn't made clear is that with the acquisition of the item comes the maintenance for it and *that* piece of information is, surprisingly, left out of the enticing equation. If you order something as common as a pizza, you have to manage it. You will eat the pizza, but to do it right you will also need plates, napkins and a perhaps a beer. If you don't use plates and napkins you'll need sponges and a wash cloth. Maintenance can't be avoided!

The acquisition of Money has maintenance attached to it as well. Once you get it, you have to *do* something with it. You are faced with many choices. You may receive money in the form of an automatic transfer (invisible!) a check, cash, or as an exchange. You will likely have to pay taxes on what you receive. (That's maintenance!)

Not setting money aside for taxes has been the downfall of many. It simply didn't occur to them that they owe The Government a share of their income. So, they spent what they had and when it came time to pay the piper they didn't have the fare. Non-payment of taxes incurs hefty fines, penalties and a big red flag on your future earnings. A vicious cycle erupts that is very difficult to break. Death and Taxes; It's no wonder they are sistered.

To prosper it is essential that you take firm hold of your financial life and plan *intelligent* management. Some people come by this skill almost automatically. They are most likely a "born-organized person."[1] Disorganized people aren't bad people, they just don't think to put things in order. They think about having fun, living in the moment and they usually don't give much credence to planning ahead. Gratification in the moment is all that matters. If they could only learn to live in the moment as well as plan for the future they'd be model people.

Are you a budget maker or a budget dodger? No matter which you are; the next task is to create a realistic budget for yourself. Oh I know you probably hate this process, and you've been hoping it wouldn't come up, but here it is nonetheless. Actually it's a very simple process and you'll love the clarity it brings into your life as well as the fresh breath of air that tags along. Budget items can line up nicely with the categories you use for your tax return; or you can use a *very* simple method of keeping track like the one I have created for you on the following page:

[1] Pam Young & Peggy Jones, "The Sidetracked Home Executives."

Allocation for a Simple Budget :
 Shelter:
 Clothing:
 Food:
 Savings:
 Medical:
 Insurances:
 Taxes
 Transportation:
 Education:
 Charity:
 Entertainment:

If you really desire wealth you must start with a budget. Skip it and you'll lack a major tool for managing your financial life. Here's what you do: Take a blank sheet of paper and create two columns. On one side list your Income (wages, salary, tips, add any other income). On the other side list your Outgo. (The eleven categories above fall into the Outgo.) In the Outgo category include how much it costs you for the space you live in. Include your rent, your mortgage, your condo fees, your property taxes, your gardener, your maintenance, your improvements, any and all outflow related to your shelter.

Clothing needs to be budgeted and the budget abided by. If you want absolute clarity, take a few moments to tally up what you spent last year so you have an idea where your money goes. Then, set an amount you are willing to spend in the coming year and don't exceed it. Remember the in and out rule: If you bring something new in, something old must go out. (More on this in Chapter Fourteen on "Balance".)

Food, whether for daily sustenance or entertainment, still requires budgeting. Allocate some of your food money to entertainment, but do it sparingly and with full knowledge that this is one area where you can get side-tracked. You need to eat, but you don't need to single handedly subsidize the restaurant industry. Without adding a tip you pay 400-500% over the food value when you eat in most moderately priced restaurants. Do you even remember what you ate two weeks ago? Probably not, but it is also likely you haven't received the bill for it yet if you put it on your credit card. Restaurant food, while it is fun to indulge in, is a seriously diminished item of return.

Saving is the key to your prosperity. And, it may not be what you think it is. "Save" is a verb meaning "to release, to free". When we save our money we release it to propagate, to compound and to increase. Saving money is the ultimate act of faith. When you *save* you free your share of money to be used by the collective for *its* increase. You demonstrate your faith that you are abundant, have plenty and, simultaneously, you demonstrate faith in your Universe for its growth and prosperity. Saving money is a highly spiritual act. Often saving is attributed to the miserly or to Scrooge-like characters. On the contrary, saving money stimulates and enhances your life and your world. It advances and affirms life. Every time you save money you are saying "yes" to life. Budget more "yeses!" in your week.

As your assets grow you will need to protect them from predators. Medical insurance is necessary to help guard your growing gold. Agents and underwriters are becoming exceedingly creative these days and they are happy to help you find a policy with appropriate coverage for you needs. Unless your job provides it, it is imperative that you include medical insurance in your budget. You need to have coverage in case of mishap. An uninsured medical emergency has left many in debt for decades. A key aspect of looking at job placement is to weigh the salary against the benefits provided. It may be worth taking a lower paying job if it offers better health premiums. You can do the math yourself, but please consider all of the possibilities before you accept a position.

Insurance is a secure way of preserving your resources. I was seriously delighted with how affordable my home, properties, and multiple auto insurances became when I gathered them under one large policy. For several weeks I received refund checks because I was qualifying for new discounts with each additional item I insured. It was a pleasant surprise to be rewarded for my customer loyalty and my *faith* in a particular insurance company. That faith was justified for me because of a wind-driven act of God.

Two days after Christmas last year, 80 mph winds toppled an eighty foot pine tree from my neighbor's yard onto my vacation home. It severed the top floor in half. Fortunately no one was home at the time and no life was lost, but the house was split in two. The insurance coverage on the home was ample enough to cover all of the losses, construction, refurbishment, moving, storage and clean up. I remember being grateful to have had the support of the field agent as well as the agent who sold me the policy. They were both in my corner and handled the claim quickly and professionally. Up until then I didn't give much thought to the insurance, the company, or the value of the policy. It was just there. I certainly appreciate it now. The house was restored and I am thankful for the insurance which covered the misfortune. Without it, I would have had to diminish my accumulated wealth in order to restore the home. Nature created a challenge and I was ready for it by way of insurance coverage.

There is another reason to carry insurance: to protect your accumulated assets. Accidents, incidents, tax and legal issues account for many lost fortunes because people were vulnerable. For many of you this is not news; but for those of you who go blithely through life humming "It's never going to happen to me," be advised that it is only wise to cover your assets completely, or you may encounter the painful life lessons of improper exposure. Okay, bad joke, but please, don't ignore the importance of having insurance.

You need to be thoroughly fiscally responsible if you intend to keep your wealth. Do not fail to file and pay your taxes on time. The IRS can take your assets, impound your paycheck, and make your financial plans implode in an instant if you do not follow their rules and calendar. While they may be lovely people as individuals, as a group they have a different agenda from yours.

Transportation is a category that should be creative. I have personally never wanted a car payment, so I've paid cash for all my cars. I'm not against payments, but I do believe the interest can be used in more productive ways. I created a fund to save towards a car. It was like having a car payment, only I was depositing three or four hundred dollars a month into my car fund. That fund grew with interest and when I had enough to purchase the car I wanted, I went out made a great cash deal, and drove home in my new car. You can save loads of money by purchasing a pre-owned vehicle. The times I have done that, I have never been unhappy. In fact, I was pleasantly surprised at the savings I made and the quality of the car I was able to afford for the price. Pre-owned can be a great bargain; just be sure to have the car checked out and insist on getting the Carfax report.

You may want to handle your transportation differently, but it is good to keep in mind that a decade from now, you'll probably have forgotten what you drove ten years back. Unless you are a car collector, opt for a reliable, moderately-priced vehicle. Do your homework and save as much as you can on a less expensive model. Be sure to figure maintenance into your transportation costs. Surprises can catch you off-guard and throw your budget out of whack. A rule of thumb is: for routine auto maintenance add $300 per year. If the car is 3 years old or more, put 10% of the value of the car into a repair fund each year. Don't forget to budget an amount for fuel.

The key to success with any budget lies in sticking to it and only spending what you have allotted for each category. If this means sharing a car, then do that. If it means taking public transportation, then do that. Do not exceed what is in your budget. Your future wealth depends on your willingness to be creative today. Transform your thoughts of inconvenience into awareness of opportunity. You never know who you will meet or what fortune will place in your path if you are willing to compromise and be creative. Some very interesting people ride the bus these days; it's become the *green thing* to do.

There may be time when you want to take a specialized course, apply for an advanced degree, or generally improve your knowledge and skills. Set up a fund to allow for your continuing education. If you can put away twenty or thirty dollars a week, you can build towards earning the degree you want. Thinking back to the "latte factor" choose to spend your money on yourself the smart way. You can easily fritter away thirty bucks a week on fancy coffee, or you can put that money into an education fund and pay for your advanced degree. The best investment you can ever make is in yourself. It is no secret that education begets opportunity in our society. Many professions require continuing education credits to retain licensure. You can always make a life, a living, and a fortune without an education, but should you choose to go the route of pursuing a higher education, you'll want to keep a liquid fund so you can accomplish that dream.

My father did exactly that. He had been a lieutenant, but not a pilot, in the Air Force. Flying was his secret dream. He had a little fund set aside for flying lessons. One day he had enough to begin his lessons and off he went. That went so well he created another little fund which he set aside for the purchase of a single engine plane. He was able to buy that too, once he got his license. Remember this was a man who worked for someone else, cared for his family and was still able to afford his dreams. He was not rich by the standards of great wealth, but he planned ahead and always got what he wanted.

Maintain separate funds for different things. If you want to save money for a vacation, open an account and deposit a certain amount into it regularly. Watch it grow and enjoy the interest building each month. NEVER use those funds for anything other than that which you intended. *Never!* Not even for emergencies. Once money has been designated for something, leave it alone. Create as many accounts as you need. Create an "emergency" fund if you like. Add money to it and watch it grow. But never get sloppy and use the "vacation" fund for your holiday presents. Using one for the other robs Peter to pay Paul and creates a negative pattern around the money. You might not think so, but it does. "Oh," you might think to yourself, "I'll just borrow a few hundred dollars from my _____ account and pay it back in two months when I'm really flush." Wanna bet? You're kidding yourself, unless you really are *that* disciplined. While your intentions may be honorable, your follow through may lack perfection. NO DIPPING. That's the rule. Stay out of your own cookie jar until your fund is at the level you want it to be. All my life I've kept separate funds for different desires. I have a vacation fund, I have an auto fund, I have a "wish list" fund for home improvements, I have no problem watching those accounts grow. I stick with my system even now.

One year I was facing paying taxes on some stocks I sold. It was a late-in-the-year transaction and I didn't want to liquidate other stocks to pre-pay the taxes. When April 15 came around I knew I'd owe a certain amount of tax on the transaction. I was tempted to "borrow" the money from my vacation fund, but I stopped myself short knowing that it could easily slip my mind and there I'd be, wanting or needing a vacation and the money was in the IRS instead of in my bank. I came up with two options: 1) I could *borrow* the money from my vacation fund provided I would draw up a contract for the loan and pay it back as I would any other bill. I could create monthly payment coupons and use them and I would pay the loan back *with* interest – to myself. I would set the interest one point above prime rate as a reminder that I'm going against my discipline. I could only use that money on the condition that I would agree with myself to set up an automatic payment (checking account debit) directly into that savings account each month, or: 2) I could borrow the money from a real bank.

I decided not to become my own lender. I didn't want to establish that tradition. I applied for a personal line of credit from the bank and let them bill me monthly. I was motivated to pay this loan back as quickly as I could and, at the same time, extricate myself from the bookwork of billing myself. In the long run I was actually saving one point of interest that I would have charged myself for the special circumstance of borrowing money from a designated account.

Sound insane? It may to you, but this rigorous discipline of account management has worked for me. It keeps money clean, clear and designated. I save myself from being disappointed when I can't take the vacation I'd been saving towards because I used the fund for something else. I also like that it keeps me honest with myself. I guess you could say I'm managing my own emotional playground by avoiding disappointment caused by my own actions. The balance of exchange comes from a sense of respect I was taught to have for money. When you designate a fund for a certain purpose, the capital in that account understands the intention and grows in accordance with your excitement. Wouldn't it be fun to withdraw your vacation savings knowing that it was just as excited as you are about making the trip?

I understand you may be feeling that there is a great deal of work and a huge commitment of time to manage money. So many little *thises and thats* to deal with. The answer is: yes and no. Once you establish your budget, your plans, your routine and your special accounts, it's all downhill. Don't worry about having a lot of little accounts. Once you develop the practice of saving, it will become a habit and you will enjoy reading your monthly growth or quarterly savings statements. Opening your bank statement will become a joyous affair.

I have a lot of practice with my diversified accounts, so now I use one large high yield money market account to combine my smaller funds and I tabulate my contributions and their earnings by way of a *split accounting tab* in my Quicken Account Manager. If you make choices to preserve your income in the very beginning watch how easily that pattern becomes habit. You'll get excited about putting money in your "special" account and when that vacation fund is full and ready, you'll really be on your way. *Aloooooha OY!*

Dedicate a specific time each week to the management of your money. It's not something you can avoid and do only once a year. Create the time to manage your wealth. Check on your accounts. Balance your books, tally your deposits; pay your bills, and pay them on time. Many highly conscious people create a ritual around this practice. Some write positive affirmations on their out-going payments. Others see the money flowing out of their account and into the universe doing good, stimulating the economy and helping others. Rituals empower thoughts as well as actions; feel free to create some of your own.

My best friend Peggy sent pictures of a particularly beautiful cat out with her bills one month. She had extra photos from a project she was doing, so she slipped a cat picture into each bill she paid. Some of the people who opened them actually called her and thanked her for making their day. We never know how our payment is going to affect someone else. Making sure the energy behind it is joy-filled, will make it more fun for you and may just alter another person's day.

Circulating your money is a powerful action. Engage in the process as if you were approaching something sacred, not scary. When you do that, you not only infuse it with personal intention but the world is blessed by your activity as well.

You may want some additional help in allocating your income. The following are guidelines for creating effective budgets for the different stages of your life. These payments should happen automatically and by choice. They are the wealth-building secret formula.

While you are still living at home:
For every dollar you receive, earn or are gifted:
50% goes into a savings account
40% is designated for spending (entertainment, clothing, computers)
10% is given to charity or spiritual work.

While you are at college or in graduate school:
For every dollar you receive, earn or are gifted:
25% goes into savings
65% is for food, supplies, entertainment, clothing
10 % is given to charity or spiritual work.

When you are out of school and get your first job:
For every dollar you earn or receive:
20% goes into savings
25% goes for rent
10% goes for entertainment
20% goes for utilities and living expenses
15% goes to transportation, car insurance
10% goes to charity or spiritual work.

Adhere to this formula in your early years and you will have enormous wealth when you reach your fifties. If you can save more, do that. If this formula pinches your life style a bit, so what! Do it anyway. You are extremely creative. You can figure out how to manage your life within these percentages. You are resourceful and can figure out how to get better deals, group rates, share expenses, car pool, double up, triple up and do whatever it takes to advance your principal. The more you can save early on, the better off you will be in later years. Money managers are telling their clients to plan for the future and plan to live until you're ninety or beyond. With those stats, you better get busy managing your money. And it is never too early (or too late) to start.

Tips on money management come in all shapes and sizes. If you need more guidance there are shelves full of books you can read on the subject. Suze Orman is one of the best teachers. "Personal Finance For Dummies" is also a great starter book. Money management does not require a sophisticated financial education. The basics are all you ever need to manage your assets. Your investment will be under twenty dollars.

Additional Tips For Acquiring and Protecting Your Principal:

Make sure you have adequate insurance. As I mentioned earlier in this chapter, insurance protects your assets in case of disaster. You want to have a policy covering auto, health, homeowner's/renter's, and property insurance. You *must* find a way to fit those payments into your budget.

Before you take a job, or interview for one, thoroughly research both the pay scale *and* the benefit scale and then work your numbers. Figure out, long before you meet your prospective employer what you will have to live on and create your budget before the appointment. Factor in the benefits that are offered. If you know before going in how much you need to earn to cover rent and how much you have allocated for transportation, it will give you a clearer idea of how you will feel about accepting this employment offer and how to negotiate your salary from a place of wisdom and strength.

It is a given that when you accept the job you will do more than you are asked to. You will be filled with the spirit of cooperation and you will know how to make the company more prosperous and meaningful in the commercial community. Before your interview research the company. Know who the executives are, read the company mission statement, understand the direction in which it is headed. When you sit down for the interview tell them how you can help them achieve their goals. You'll get the job if you put the priorities of the company first. You'll have time to ask questions about your salary and benefits later. Show them what you can do for them and when you get the job, remain in that mindset every day. Remember how my mother diligently turned her small town part-time job into a lucrative career and, ultimately, store ownership.

When you are employed for more than six months there are generally bonuses awarded at the holidays and for exceptional performance. What do you do with your bonus? Or, what if you have inherited a bequest from your Great Aunt Lucy? What you must do in the future is save it. My friend the bartender created his real estate fortune by saving his tips. He built it one dollar at a time. So must you. If you are tempted to blow that bonus on some trinket, or take a trip, wait. Put it into your principal account. If you want to take part of it and put that into your travel account, okay. But make it a reasonable amount, 30% would be fair, but not more. If you hold your horses and let it grow, you'll be able to take fifty trips later on. Plan ahead to save all of your unexpected income.

Clothing is another way you can save a bundle. The son of a very wealthy business friend of mine told me an amazing story. He attended college in San Francisco and to save money, he made his own clothes. His parents allocated a certain amount for him as a monthly living expense. He decided he wanted to live beneath his means and save for the future. He bought a second hand sewing machine and tailored his clothing from purchases he made at thrift stores.

Every cent he got he saved. When he had saved enough, he purchased his first piece of real estate in San Francisco. He paid for the refurbishment of it out of his savings and rented it as soon as it was completed. With a steady rent coming in he was soon able to find a second piece of property and do the same thing. He always looked presentable, clean, and while not as stylish as the cover of GQ Magazine, he was certainly acceptable. After 10 years of wisely managing his real estate acquisitions, he is worth millions. He doesn't make his own clothing anymore and he is able to shop at the finest stores, but he could make them again if he needed to. He started out no more privileged than most of us.

I love this story because it demonstrates exactly where his priorities were. He wanted to save, amass, and build his financial base. He did that by making choices about his college allowance and living expenses, spending, self-gratification, and forgettable purchases. He and his young family are now assured a solid financial future.

Which brings me to this point: Most of us don't need as many clothes as we have: Narrow your wardrobe down to the basics, buy the best quality you can afford, buy long-lasting and not trendy, and maintain what you do have until you replace it. One rule to live by is to never buy anything new until you're ready to recycle something in your closet. If you want to buy a new sweater; an old one has to go. This way you can keep a handle on your closet and reduce the clutter and help to stop the plague of consumerism we see in this country.

"But, what if something unexpected happens. What will I do then?" you ask. The rule always applies: We never deplete principal even on special occasions. We leverage it instead. If you have a growing amount in the bank or a money market or CD account, you can borrow money using this as collateral. Although it may appear strange to do this, the act of borrowing accomplishes two things: it establishes you as a worthy creditor and it challenges you to find creative ways to pay off the emergency and still live beneath your means. You will want the *worthy creditor* title when you are ready to purchase a home, or apply for a business loan. It is never too early to establish a credit rating and a flawless record of payments. Leaving your principal intact allows you to leverage it. Once you erode your principal, you have damaged your wealth.

The last point for Management is to get professional help when you need it. Once you have passed a savings mark of $20,000, start interviewing financial planners and money managers. Purchase a book or two on investing so you'll have a working knowledge of the terms. "Investing for Dummies" is a great beginning. Be conversant in terms. You don't have to know everything in detail, but having an understanding of stocks, bonds, annuities, and margins is a good beginning. Pick a financial manager who will help you build your future. They should ask you what YOU want to accomplish. They should be willing to forecast and chart the growth of your capital. You should ask them about their commission formula (on both the buy and the sell end) and you should always insist on a diversified portfolio.

I work with a financial planner who was one of the few that didn't have revenue loss in the technology stock market crash of the mid-nineties. Many investors lost huge amounts of capitol when the high tech stocks and the dot coms lost value. Her clients were well diversified and balanced, and when the devaluation came; those portfolios absorbed the storm more easily than those who were heavily invested in high tech. Don't be afraid to ask for help.

Please don't try to navigate the stock market alone; no matter what the late-night infomercials may promise you. Unless you are highly trained this is a field only for specialists. Plenty of do-it-yourself "day traders" have become night-time shreikers due to the losses they have sustained while impersonating a savvy stock broker.

Interview several financial planners. Be clear about your financial goals, "I want to have _____money by the time I'm _____(age.)" See what they offer you. This is your future. It is your life; you are entitled to shop around for the right person to be your partner in money management. Show this person the Money Model you are working with. Divulge your strategy. If they negate it, walk away. If they embrace it, ask them for a few references from their current clients and make the calls. Trusting your wealth to someone else is an intimate relationship. Ask his or her clients about any questions or insecurities you are feeling. Most people are happy to help and if they are pleased with the service they are receiving, happy to recommend. Be sure to do your research, it will save you sorrow later on. Once you have selected the person you want to entrust as your co-manager, don't just walk away whistling Dixie. It is still your responsibility to regularly review your monthly statements and to ask questions if you don't understand something. Remember: the financial planner works for you.

You will need to keep an eye out for yourself when it comes to charges, fees and commissions. Take the time to review your statements when you pay your bills. When you make it a regular part of your financial management evening, and you do it on a regularly scheduled basis, you're becoming a true resource manager.

One final thought before we move onto the next chapter. Please remember that none of the people I use as examples have had anything to work with but ordinary income. None of us had exceptionally lucrative jobs. Each person simply managed the resources that they earned. You can do it too. Just follow the advice in this book, do the work, and when the time comes, get professional help to co-manage your prosperity. This is the map to your personal gold mine.

Fortune is not something to find but to unfold.
– Eric Butterworth

Chapter Thirteen
Lesson 12:
Contribution

Treat people as if they were what they ought to be
and you help them to become
what they are capable of being.
– Goethe

One of the most important first steps you will ever take in the Money Model of Management is to define and designate your endowments to charity. **Contribution** is a two-fold concept: it is what you bring to the world in the form of your gifts and talents and it is also the seed of essential giving back which we all must do to maintain our integrity as participants in the spectrum of life.

What do you bring to the party of life? Surely you have a sense of your specialties – those things you do exceptionally well that others appreciate; or do you allow yourself to be taken for granted and just do what you're pushed into doing? Although Contribution appears to be the last on the list for the Money Model, it actually is one of the most significant considerations.

To understand the full measure of contribution, you'll first need to identify your unique special gifts and talents. If you're comfortable and familiar with knowing and identifying them, make a list of your Top Twelve talents (in no particular order). When you've done that, call/email/fax your list to a friend and ask them to rate the items based on a scale of *one to ten*, one being the highest. When they return the list, compare it to your list and consider the insights you have gained. (If this is done correctly two qualities/talents will not be rated.) If they are willing to help you further, ask them to send you what they think are your Top *Three* talents, whether they are on your original list or not.

If you don't have a clue where to begin then I encourage you to perform this exercise first:

> *Close your eyes. Sit back and take a few deep breaths*
> *to relax your mind and body.*

Imagine an award ceremony in progress. Place it in a fantasy setting. Picture the person handing out the awards. What are they wearing? What are the colors of the space? What is the temperature, what are the scents and the sounds? You hear your name called. You some forth and are presented an award for one of your talents. What is the award for? How do you accept that award? Do you speak? Do you thank someone or something? Your name is called again and you are given a second award. What is this award for. How do you respond? You return to your place and your name is called once again. As you approach the award giver, what are your thoughts? The awards are mounting. You are given a fourth award. Describe what this one is for? How are you feeling? You are called again, this time there is wild support in the space for you. You have been given a fifth award for one of your talents. How do you respond? As you return to your place in the room see the five awards gleaming. They all have your name on them. As you stand among them how do you respond to these accolades? Take a few moments to dwell in this surrounding. When you've taken the moment, open your eyes and list the five awards.

When you've completed this exercise, continue with your list until you have written down twelve talents/qualities in all . Then call your friend for input. When you have received the feedback from your friend, you will have a very clear idea of how the outside world views your talents and your contributions to the planet. Look to your talents as the means by which you receive remuneration on tangible, as well as intangible, levels. When you receive through these channels, the return is immeasurable.

Talents are bestowed upon us freely by the enthusiastic spirit of Universal generosity. We are given these attributes so that we might use them to significant advantage. Our talents move us along our path and allow us to receive an inflow of positive energy (money, compliments, accolades, appreciation). These talents also enhance the world when we share them generously with family, community and society. If we are holding back or stifling our gifts we are creating a stoppage in the flow of prosperity that may come into our lives.

114

Contribution is a very simple method of *priming the pump* of our prosperity. Those who work the land understand the need to prime the pump. The process requires that you fill the flow pipes with a small amount of water and *coax* the pump into starting up. It is literally tickled into action by sensing a flow and responds by pumping more, supplying more, water. Farmers use this technique for irrigation and it is also employed for moving water from one place to another via a pipe and pump assembly. The point is to increase the flow of water into the area you designate. We definitely want an open flow of riches into our lives. The flow begins when we prime the prosperity pump.

How do your prime your prosperity pump? Certainly by contributing to society, but also by setting aside some of your income to subsidize the resources you value. For many people this takes the form of a church or religious organization. For others there are an array of social charities, international funds, teams that help humanity and thousands of other groups with a mission to help.

The Old Testament commanded that ten percent of a person's resources had to be given to support the work of the temple. Instead of being bound by an ancient law, create your own open line of heart-felt, spirit-filled and money-backed subsidy for those persons, places and things that provide value and inspiration to you and to others.

Contribution must come from an inner place of true generosity. It cannot be begrudged, commanded, demanded, or given with any type of negative thought or emotion attached to it; it must be surrendered confidently and in total trust. You always can reserve the right to designate what those funds will be used for. Designate though, don't dictate.

The rule I have enjoyed following in my personal life is that of random contribution. I vary the charities each year, adding some and switching some around. Depending on what is happening in the world I might give to a relief fund after a natural disaster, or I might continue contribution to the agencies that consistently provide relief no matter what or where the challenge.

My contributions are usually over the ten per cent mark. Sometimes the designated funds go directly to friends that have suffered losses and need financial relief. Sometimes the contributions go to help animal rights and animal preservation. Other times I'll give to medical research; other times to free clinics providing medical aid. My giving varies; sometimes it is planned, sometimes it is spontaneous, it is never over-looked. A friend asked me once how to manage all of the requests that come in, especially all of the special funds and disaster relief work that so tug at the heart. I told her to budget a regular amount from her salary and to designate the charities she gives to; then set aside about ten percent of that amount for the unexpected. Following this formula, you can have the best of both worlds. Your special charities and churches will be able to count on your regular donation, and you will be able to help in those emergencies when they arise. Contribution doesn't have to be an exact science but the funds for it, like everything else in your life, must be managed and set aside.

Contribution is ultimately about circulation. The word *circulation* derives' from "circle". What goes around; comes around. If we want more we must keep the giant whisk stirring the pot of prosperity, even if we *think* we need the money more than *they* do, because, if we think that way, we will.

Life, like a mirror, never gives back
more than we put into it.
– Anonymous

Chapter Fourteen
Lesson 13:
Balance

> *Wealth is the ability to fully experience life.*
> – Henry David Thoreau

You have nearly competed your guided tour around The Money Model. The center square, Balance, is the pivot point of The Money Model. It supplies the power and the purpose for the rest. **Balance** is how we keep our money, our health, our loves, our work, our dreams and our entire life, not just in perspective, but also in congruency. There's that word again: congruency! And please note, congruency is only possible when we achieve Balance.

Balance appears at the very center of our Money Model. It is no mistake that it touches all of the other squares that comprise the Model. Balance is the core of wealth and prosperous living.

> *Happiness is not a matter of intensity but of*
> *balance, order, rhythm and harmony.*
> – Thomas Merton

Balance is common vernacular. We *balance* our checkbook, *balance* our tires, gymnasts walk a *balance* beam, we create a *balanced* diet, we *balance* work and play, and we understand the political theories behind a *balance* of power in Washington.

Balance is an instrument for determining weight, an ideal for international trade, a Van Halen album, and award-winning film short, an accounting term, the knob on a stereo which governs volume, the composition and placement of items in an art piece which produces an aesthetically pleasing experience, a wheel that regulates the beats of a clock, and the weighing of all possibilities in a given situation. Balance has a large agenda to fulfill.

Let's look more closely at how *Balance* applies to your prosperity and why it is the center of the Money Model.

For the linquists in the world: Balance comes from the Latin word "bi-lanx" meaning two plates (for weighing). From Latin we got "balancia," and now modern day balance. Picture the Scales of Justice and you'll see balance. It's all about making things *right* and *even.*

Without balance, we run the risk of taking on too much of a thing, bloating with excess and ultimately self destructing; or at least being decidedly uncomfortable. Balance creates a needed exchange between acquisition and contribution, so that we don't horde and stagnate. If we have understanding but no discipline, we will not hold onto our assets. Likewise, if we have principles but do not engage in proper management, our financial life will lack focus and run amok. Being the center square, Balance creates the essential energetic interaction to achieve perspective and equality among all of the segments of the Money Model.

Balance has a huge assignment. It looks after all the parts of what it is involved with and brings them into symmetry. Balance is responsible for harmony, happiness and all that we strive for, without it we disintegrate.

The major components of Balance in your Money Model are:

Weight
Measure
Allocation
Desire
Control

Weight: Everything you think and do has importance attached to it. In the scale of your life what carries weight for you? What *weighs* on your mind and drives your choices?

Measure: The means by which you weigh the options and make a decision. Measure is also the art of taking a little from one square or another to even-out the distribution of material things. One area should not be heaver than another, so you proportion your attention to each square to achieve equilibrium.

Allocation: How you distribute the load among the squares. You alone decide which area gets what and how much. You also decide the amount and the ratio.

118

Desire: Fuels your fire for prosperity. You aspire to have a certain life and style. This desire propels you through the rough days and provides the way you to come to terms with the requirements for achieving your ambitions. Desire is the essential emotional component for balance to reach its nadir.

Control: You are the sole and complete Master of your Money Model. No one else can control it or your resources. Single-handedly, you oversee and manage it in order to create the results you want. Control is the ultimate end all and be all, the secret to the whole ball of wax.

One example of balance in action: You decide to go shopping for a new sweater. You have checked your budget and you can spend $50. Before you purchase a new sweater, an old, tired one has to be recycled or donated. Before you add anything into your life, something else must go. That's what we call true balance. Try it.

When you practice this technique you will cherish what you have even more. Not only will you be participating in global conservation, you will be living in a harmony of exchange that circulates the wealth. No more consumption for the sake of consumption; your new life embraces a changed way of thinking and acting which, in turn, fosters mindful living through balance.

Utilize balance in working through the Money Model and you will have wealth. Apply the principle of balance to the other segments of your life and you will have bliss.

*The true definition of balance is having a
cookie in each hand.*
–Anonymous

Chapter Fifteen
Strawberry Fields Forever

You've come full circle, or full square if we are true to the Money Model. You've learned the underlying truths about money, the maxims for managing it, the invisible laws that govern it and now you're ready to begin your personal path to wealth. Congratulations. You've faced your fears, you've girded your loins (what a trooper) and you've fastened your seat belt. From this point on, you're seizing the day and slaying the dragon of days gone by. Whew! It sounds like you've accomplished a Herculean task.

It doesn't have to be. It can be very simple. Allow me one more story about my mentor, my father, as an example.

When my parents moved to the Northwest they rented an apartment for the first couple years. One Sunday, they went for a sight-seeing tour and discovered a nifty neighborhood on top of a hill which had a panoramic view of the bay and local islands. Houses and well-manicured gardens dotted the crest of the hill. My dad, who was just starting out, didn't have the down payment for a house, but he spotted a piece of land he thought would be a dandy location for a house...that he, of course, following in his parent's footsteps, would build.

A friendly neighbor informed my dad that a guy named "Boots," who lived in the gray house on the corner, owned the land. My ever-enterprising dad knocked on his door. A cranky old man who did not enjoy being disturbed on a Sunday by anyone, let alone a stranger, greeted him. "What do you want?" he growled. The conversation was brief. My dad inquired about purchasing the land below the old man's house. "Those are my strawberries," he said, " and I'm not them selling to anyone." The door slammed shut. Politely, my dad took his leave and nothing more was said about the land until six months later.

Another Sunday drive resulted in another knock at the old man's door and the reception was predictably as frigid. This time though, my dad threw out a number as an offer and "Boots" said he'd think about it. Another six months passed, another Sunday drive begat another knock. This time the answer was, "Call me tomorrow." My dad, the tenacious leprechaun, was thrilled.

Monday morning came and he made the call. Two weeks later we were the proud owners of a strawberry field which had a panoramic ocean view. The berry thing seems to be a recurring theme.

Meticulously, my parents planned to build their dream house. They made a list of every step in the process and attached an estimated cost to each feature. My father wanted to do as much of the labor as he could to save expenses. The rest he and the contractor would negotiate. The contractor bulldozed the land and laid the concrete foundation; my dad built the frame, installed all the plumbing and wired in the electrical connections. Then, the contractor came behind him with drywall and plaster.

I was five when my parents were building our house. Every evening after work, it was a ritual. My dad would come home, grab a fast dinner, change out of his suit, collect my mother and me and up the hill we'd go. My dad strapped on his tool belt and went to work. He sawed, hammered, nailed and framed. I can still recall the smell of damp, freshly cut lumber as if it were yesterday. My mother helped. She steadied the lumber for his saw; she held the tools for him and she watched me so I didn't fall into something and crack it or my head. Often my dad would show me how to do something, too. We played "witch" while he was plumbing the house. A propane stove he carried with him fired his cast iron pot of molten lead. When the lead was all melty and red, he would stir it with his cast iron ladle and we'd both pretend we were witches. "Heh, heh, heh," we'd say over the bubbling pot. Just about that time my mother would find us and ask my father what kind of nonsense he was teaching me. Our game was over for the night. Our magic elixir was poured onto the pipes to seal them against leaks. As the pot dwindled, my eyes drooped and I fell asleep in my little sleeping bag as they worked later into the night.

Night after night, and on weekends they worked. My dad taught my mother how to wire an electrical outlet into a wall. He taught her how to plumb and prime the joints to be sealed with molten lead. He taught her how to solder and how to drill. She was his right hand and more.

My folks only spent what they could save. If they didn't have enough for the next stage, they waited until they did. The contractor was very impressed with my dad, so much so that occasionally he'd complete a stage on his own and defer the payment until later. It was his way of supporting my dad in his dream.

It took a little over a year to complete the house. I remember the day it was finished. The neighbors joined in for a congratulatory picnic. The rooms were bare, the walls needed paint and carpets were lacking, but there was joy, pride of accomplishment, and, best of all, no mortgage.

Suddenly, we had our own house. When it was completed it was quite the showplace. My dad, as you recall, was an electrical engineer and a designer. He installed a switch in the bedroom that would turn on the coffee pot in the kitchen every morning. These were the fifties, no one else had such clever timers. He could orchestrate the exterior floodlights from his bedside. He had switches that turned the fireplace on, he had switches that illuminated the carport, he had switches that turned on the radiant ceiling heat, and he even had a switch that would turn on the space heater to warm up the cold bathroom tile. He had relay switches, dimmers, and time-delay lights for entering and exiting the house. He was amazing. You can imagine what he was able to do at Christmas!

He hauled the slate from the quarry to make the fireplace in the living room and he built a stone wall in the front yard which he collected rock by rock. There was no end to his industry and his hard work.

Every night he came home and celebrated our castle. The whole family built it. Even my five year old fingers had a touch in that house. The lessons he lived by served him well and have served me, too. I hope you can apply them and prosper.

If there is one statement my father would want to pass along to you it would be Samuel Johnson's admonition: "Clear your mind of *can't*" Go out and find your strawberry field. Build the house of your dreams and create the wealth you deserve. My father's Gold Mind was exemplified by the strawberry field. He prospected until he struck gold, and when he did he created more and more abundance for himself and for others.

Now, you have all the secrets to do the same for yourself. From my family to yours, with love.

*Children are the living messages we send
to a time we will not see.*
Neil Postman

My parents, Maureen and Vernon Young, on their wedding day in Australia and later on the front porch of my grandparents' home in Potlatch, Idaho.

Suggested Further Reading:

Eric Butterworth:
www.ericbutterworth.com
> *Spiritual Economics*

Terry Cole-Whittaker:
www.TerryColeWhittaker.com
> *Dare to be Great*
> *How to Have More in a Have-Not World*
> *What You Think of Me is None of My Business*

Suze Orman:
www.suzeorman.com
> *Women & Money*
> *Road to Wealth*
> *Financial Guidebook*

Deepak Chopra:
www.chopra.com
> *The Seven Spiritual Laws of Success*

George Weinberg
> *Self Creation*

Wallace D. Wattles:
www.wallacewattles.com
> *The Science of Getting Rich*

Catherine Ponder
> T*he Dynamic Laws of Prosperity*

Dr. Frederick Eikerenkoetter (Rev. Ike):
www.revike.org
> *Health, Happiness and Prosperity - For YOU*

Appendix A
The Money Model

Inspiration for the Money Model came to me while studying the 5,000 year old Chinese practice of Form School Feng Shui. The Chinese believed that if all nine sections of your life were in balance you would experience success and happiness. If one of the areas of your life was out of balance, or in distress, then you would experience lack. The practice of Feng Shui teaches that by laying a map of all nine areas over your home you can make changes and modifications that will increase the positive flow of Ch'i (life force) and enhance your life. The nine squares, include every area that has importance to your life: Career, Knowledge & Self Cultivation, Health & Family, Wealth & Prosperity, Fame & Reputation, Love & Marriage, Creativity & Children, Helpful People & Travel, and finally the Center. The center square touches on every other square thereby affecting and being affected by all of the sections. For 5,000 years this art and science has been successfully practiced. If we apply this same powerful structure to our financial life we can shift it by managing each of the nine qualities of financial balance and health.

The Chinese Feng Shui Chart

WEALTH	FAME	LOVE
HEALTH	CENTER	CREATIVITY
SELF	CAREER	BENEFACTORS

ENTRANCE

You can learn more about Feng Shui by purchasing my book "Feng Shui the Easy Way."

Appendix B:
Our Staggering Individual and National Debt

• Total US consumer debt (which includes installment debt, but not mortgage debt) reached $2.46 Trillion in June 2007, up from $2.398 Trillion at the end of 2006 (Source: Federal Reserve)

• Total US consumer revolving debt reached $904 Billion in June 2007, up from $879 billion at the end of 2006 (Source: Federal Reserve)

• The median U.S. household income is currently $43,200 and the typical family's credit card balance is now almost 5 percent of their annual income. (Source: Federal Reserve)

• Of the households that do owe money on credit cards, the median balance was $2,200 — meaning that half owe more, and half less. (Source: MSN Money)

• 8.3 percent of households owe $9,000 or more on their cards (Source: MSN Money)

• Approximately 40 percent of credit card users paid their balance in full each month in 2006 (Source: Federal Reserve Bank of Philadelphia)

• The majority of U.S. households have no credit card debt. About a quarter have no credit cards, and an additional 30 percent of households pay off their balances every month. (Source: Federal Reserve)

• On average, today's consumer has a total of 13 credit obligations on record at a credit bureau. These include credit cards (such as department store charge cards, gas cards or bank cards) and installment loans (auto loans, mortgage loans, student loans, etc.). Not included are savings and checking accounts (typically not reported to a credit bureau). Of these 13 credit obligations, nine are likely to be credit cards and four are likely to be installment loans. (Source: myfico.com)

• 51 percent of the US population has at least two credit cards (Source: Center for Media Research)

• Approximately 14 percent of Americans use 50 percent or more of their available credit, and this group carries an average of 6.6 credit cards (Source: Center for Media Research)

• Those utilizing at least 50 percent of their credit lines have an average credit score of 645, compared to the national average of 674 (Source: Center for Media Research)

• One in six families with credit cards pays only the minimum due every month. (Sources: American Bankers Association, Federal Reserve)

• About 40 percent of credit card holders carry a balance of less than $1,000. About 15 percent are far less conservative in their use of credit cards and have total card balances in excess of $10,000. When you look at the total of all credit obligations combined (except mortgage loans), 48 percent of consumers carry less than $5,000 of debt. This includes all credit cards, lines of credit, and loans-everything but mortgages. Nearly 37 percent carry more than $10,000 of non-mortgage-related debt as reported to the credit bureaus. (Source: myfico.com)

• The average consumer's oldest obligation is 14 years old, indicating that he or she has been managing credit for some time. In fact, we found that one out of four consumers had credit histories of 20 years or longer. Only one in 20 consumers had credit histories shorter than two years. (Source: myfico.com)

• At least one in 10 consumers have more than 10 credit cards in their wallets. However, the overall average number of credit cards per consumer is four.   (Source: Experian's "National Score Index")

• Twenty-nine percent of low and middle income households with credit card debt reported that medical expenses contributed to their current balances. (Source: www.demos.org)

• U.S. consumers racked up an estimated $51 billion worth of fast food on their personal credit and debit cards in 2006, compared to $33.2 billion one-year ago. (Source: www.carddata.com)

• Americans over 50 are more likely to have a credit card than those 25 – 49 years old, but tend to use them less frequently (Source: 2007 AARP Payments Study)

• Eighty-eight percent of consumers surveyed admitted to immediately shredding or simply throwing out credit card offers they receive in the mail (Source: GfK Roper Survey)

• Low interest rate is by far the most important factor when choosing a new credit card, cited by 58 percent of respondents (Source: GfK Roper Survey)

• Consumers carry more than 1 billion Visa cards worldwide—more than 450 million of those cards are in the United States (Source: Visa USA)

• U.S. Visa cardholders alone conduct more than $1 trillion in annual volume (Source: Visa USA)

• The average ticket for Visa purchases is consistently more than cash (Source: Visa USA)

More books from
Dr. kac young

Gold Mind: The Workbook
When you are prospecting for Gold, it helps to have a map to follow. The workbook supports you in your process of mining the gold within. It organizes your thoughts, assesses your assets, and keeps you on the track to attaining and maintaining prosperity.

Discover Your Spiritual Genius
A compendium of helpful shortcuts for your spiritual development. This is the beginner's guide to knowing it all. You need this book if you're feeling down I the dumps or if your life isn't working the way you want it to. If you read and follow this advice life will take on a new meaning, you will be on top of your game, in charge of your life, happier and more fulfilled.

Twenty-one Days to the Love of Your Life
Create the relationship of your dreams by using this proven process to attract the mate you desire. This is a powerful and success oriented process for the serious seeker who truly desires a soul-mate and life partner.

Twenty-one Days to the Love of Your Life: The Workbook
Let this workbook becomes a place to put your "love-work", a map for charting your journey to love, and a reminder of how far you've come. You can read the book and create love without it, but it makes the process clearer and more powerful.

Feng Shui, The Easy Way
The ancient art that can change your life overnight. These proven principles and practices can create immediate and powerful results. Change and shift are the natural qualities of life which you can use to your advantage through the application of Feng Shui. This easy-to-understand book explains the science and art of Feng Shui simply and clearly. You'll be able to put the information to use at once.

Dancing With the Moon
Learn how to use the natural energies of lunar forces to orchestrate your life, your emotions and to create a deeper experience of living life to its fullest measure. Dancing With the Moon is a easy process to understand and practice. You can change anything in your life by using this method of connection and collaboration with the Moon.

Star Power
Create the year you want and fulfill your dreams by working with the energies of the stars and the planets. You can create the life you have always wanted by following these 12 simple steps that are just out there waiting for you. You don't have to be an astrologer to work these steps. You just need 40 minutes a day for 12 days and you will powerfully direct your upcoming year.

Runes for Women: The Gifts of the Goddess
The ancient divination technique has a new twist: in this book it's all about women. *Runes for Women* utilizes secrets from powerful cultures, and shifts the emphasis from warrior to goddess; this is the original gift of the Runes. The Runic Oracle is as powerful today as it was hundreds of years ago, only more so because its true depth and purpose has been revealed.

Private consultation is available for any and all of these subjects. For more information contact:

Dr. kac young
PO Box 376
Cambria, CA. 93428-2004

www.spiritualgenius.com
and
www.fengshuispecialist.com
and
www.spiritualgenius.Ning.com